PVC Furniture

Edward A. Baldwin

TAB BOOKS
Blue Ridge Summit, PA

FIRST EDITION
FIRST PRINTING

© 1992 by **Edward A. Baldwin**.
Published by TAB Books.
TAB Books is a division of McGraw-Hill, Inc.

Library of Congress Cataloging-in-Publication Data

Baldwin, Edward A.
    PVC furniture / Edward A. Baldwin.
      p. cm.
    Includes index.
    ISBN 0-8306-4077-0 (h) ISBN 0-8306-4076-2 (p)
    1. Plastic furniture. 2. Plastics craft. 3. Polyvinyl chloride.
  I. Title.
  TT297.B35 1992
  684.1′06—dc20   91-45068
                                            CIP

TAB Books offers software for sale. For information and a catalog, please contact
TAB Software Department, Blue Ridge Summit, PA 17294-0850.

Acquisition Editor: Kimberly Tabor
Book Editor: Shelley Chevalier
Director of Production: Katherine G. Brown
Book Design: Jaclyn J. Boone
Cover Design: Graphics Plus, Hanover, PA   HT3

This book is dedicated with love to my daughter, Debra Ann, and her family. They, like all young families, are looking for ways to save money and furnish their home. PVC projects provide inexpensive options for furnishing your home.

Acknowledgments

Project Design: Ed Baldwin
Editorial Director: Barbara Sachs Kremer
Production Manager: Ed Baldwin
Art: Jerri Long
Decorative Folk Art: Glennda Suter
Project Materials: Genova Products, Inc.
Photography: Baldwin Publishing, Inc.
Photo Stylist: Janet Hickman
Design Consultant: Jon A. Kremer, P.E.

The projects in this book were made using a Shopsmith and hand-held power tools from Black and Decker. The router bits and saw blades were Freud products.

Contents

Introduction

If you loved playing with Legos, Tinker Toys, or an Erector set when you were a kid, you're going to have fun building PVC pipe furniture. Even if you have two left hands and no talent for construction, you're still going to enjoy working with this product. It's easy to work with. It's easy to saw, cut, and assemble. You can stain it, paint it, and even dye it in some cases. Combine it with wood and you can create a vast variety of attractive and functional indoor and outdoor furniture, birdhouses and feeders, and lots of things to use around the house. But whatever you do, read this section carefully before you begin any of the projects.

General characteristics

PVC, or polyvinyl chloride, pipe is designed for cold-water plumbing. CPVC, or chlorinated polyvinyl chloride, is designed for hot-water plumbing and is also the more expensive of the two. I found CPVC to be too yellow in color, too flexible, and much too expensive. The same size PVC is easily obtained and is pure white.

Pipe and fittings are available in two categories or types: pressure pipe and sewer pipe. Sewer pipe and fittings are less expensive than pressure pipe, but the fittings of pressure pipe are a tad bit stronger and more attractive, thus making nicer-looking furniture. For our purposes, there are two weights of pipe, schedule 40 and 80. I only used schedule 40 pressure pipe in all of the projects in this book. It's your option to use pressure fittings or sewer fittings (FIG. A).

One last observation: polypropylene and styrene are also used in the manufacture of pipe and fittings. I only use PVC pipe and fittings.

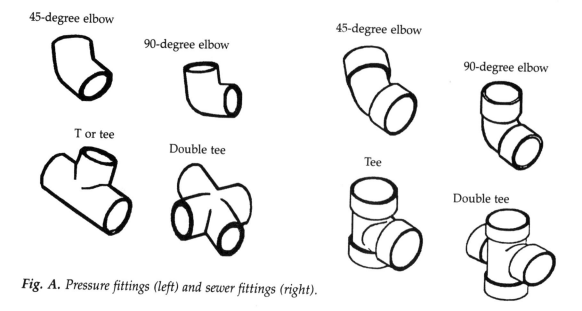

Fig. A. *Pressure fittings (left) and sewer fittings (right).*

PVC pipe strengths, weaknesses, and durability

To some extent, PVC pipe is much like human bone. It can take quite a bit of direct pressure, but will break or crack if bent too far. Extremely high temperatures will cause the pipe to soften. CPVC pipe will remain hard at higher temperatures than PVC pipe, but even PVC will withstand a hotter temperature (about 120 degrees) than your furniture would normally be exposed to, unless of course you live in an oven. Extremely low temperatures will not harm PVC pipe but can make it brittle. Under freezing conditions, a sharp knock against something hard could cause the pipe to crack or shatter. One word of caution: PVC furniture is strong, but if you have friends or relatives who weigh more than 300 pounds, you may want to offer them another chair.

The final question is one of durability. How long can you expect PVC pipe to last, especially out of doors in the rain and snow and heat of day? One argument, probably emanating from the people who sell copper pipe, says PVC pipe deteriorates when exposed to the elements. It does, and ultraviolet light is the culprit; but the deterioration happens over a very long period of time. I have a chaise I made in 1981 that is still standing on an uncovered outdoor patio. It shows no noticeable signs of deterioration. I had to replace the cushions twice, that's all. But, if you are concerned, paint the pipe (see "Finishing your PVC project" in this introduction).

Pipe and fittings sizes

I use straight pipe and fittings of various contours and shapes. The fittings are used to join the straight lengths of pipe. All of the fittings I use are of the female variety. That's a plumbing term and is not meant to raise any gender questions. The pipe is all male variety, and, while you can purchase pipe with female fittings molded into the ends, that end usually has to be discarded since it won't match the style of the other fittings. The fittings that come with collars are the sewer-pipe variety. The fittings with smooth contours are the pressure-pipe variety.

Be careful when buying the fittings. Three types of 90-degree elbows are available. One is called a standard, the other a short turn, and the last a 90-degree long sweep. I use the standard elbow. Two types of double-tee fittings are also available: a cross with shorter ends, and the standard double tee. I use the standard double tee. The other fitting frequently used is the standard tee. The type of tees and elbows are schedule 40 pressure.

Pipe and fitting sizes are sold based upon the internal diameter. A 1-inch pipe has an internal diameter of 1 inch, give or take a little (that's called the tolerance). Therein lies the problem, the variance, or the bugaboo. Because some manufacturers only make pipe and others only fittings, you'll find variations in the tolerance. Double-check the pipe and fittings for snugness of fit before leaving the store. The pipe should fit into the fitting without rocking back and forth.

PVC pipe for home use comes in sizes ranging from 1/2 inch to 6 inches. A commercial variety of pipe can be much larger. The smaller size of 1/2 to 1 inch is not strong enough to use in projects required to hold body weight, i.e., chair frame construction. Most of the pipe used for that kind of project will be 1 1/4 to 2 inches. The larger pipe can be used, but is also correspondingly expensive. I used large pipe scraps from construction jobs for some of the projects in this book.

When you begin assembly, you will insert straight pipe into fittings to form connections. The depth that the straight pipe goes into the fitting can vary, depending on the brand and type of fitting. This depth is called the fitting allowance and has already been included in the measurements given for each project. The fitting allowance used for each project is included in the materials list. This allowance also has been added to each end of the pipe lengths to be cut.

When you buy your fittings, measure inside to see how far into the fitting the pipe will go. If that distance is more (or less) than the amount listed, add (or subtract) the difference before you cut your straight pipe lengths.

Securing the joints

When a plumber puts PVC pipe together, it is supposed to hold up under pressurized conditions so your house doesn't get an unexpected wet surprise. The cements used for this purpose fuse the pipe and fittings together through a chemical reaction. Once the pipe and fitting are set, it becomes one integrated piece of pipe. There is no way to disassemble the connection short of cutting the pipe and reaming out the fitting, which is very impractical and hard to do. Unless you plan to run water through your furniture, you have no real reason to use cement, unless of course you want to. Sheet metal screws can be used to hold the pipe and fittings together, especially if you want to be able to disassemble the project at some later date (see 'Cutting and drilling PVC pipe").

If you opt to use cement, make certain the joint is clean. Use PVC pipe cleaner (see "Finishing your PVC project") for this purpose. I suggest you dry-assemble all projects and mark the fittings and pipe so that when you reassemble the project you can quickly align the pieces. This point is crucial because you only have a few seconds before the bonding action starts. Once this happens you are not going to be able to budge that joint; the bond is permanent.

In most cases you might have to sand the ends of the pipe to get a smooth insertion. Once the ends are clean, apply the cement, put the pieces together, give them a twist or two to force out any air bubbles, and you are done. *Caution:* Work in a well-ventilated area; the cement fumes are toxic.

One point to remember: Any cemented project too big to get through the doorway of the room where you made it has found a permanent home.

If you want to disassemble a project at a later date to store it or move it, you can use sheet metal screws to hold the pipe and fittings together. For example, you could cement the sides of a chair together and then use screws to hold the center pieces of pipe in place. This type of construction would allow you to knock down the chair for storage in the winter or for ease of moving.

Cutting and drilling PVC pipe

PVC pipe is normally sold in 10- and 20-foot lengths. You must cut the pipe to specified lengths for each project. If you plan to make several projects, add the lengths of the same diameter pipe pieces you'll need, and you'll eliminate having a lot of waste pipe left over. The instructions to make each project in this book include a list of the required lengths of straight pipe. The pieces are identified as P1, P2, and so on. If you label each piece as you cut it, you will know at a glance where it goes when you are in the assembly process later. Labeling can be done with a pencil, grease pencil, or felt-tipped marker. I use a grease pencil.

A handsaw (FIG. B), coping saw, hacksaw, or power saw will cut the pipe with ease. If you have access to a fine-tooth blade in a band saw, it's your best bet.

To make a nice, square 90-degree cut, wrap a piece of paper around the pipe and follow the edge of the paper with your saw. When you begin cutting, always cut the longest pieces first, followed by the second longest, etc. This way you will have less waste. You will need sandpaper or a file to smooth off burrs and rough spots from the cut ends.

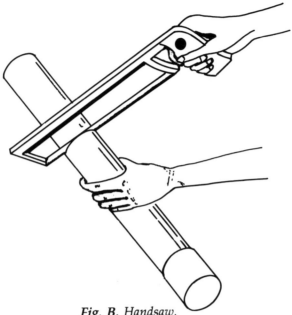

Fig. B. Handsaw.

Ratchet shears

Figure C illustrates a gizmo called ratchet shears, specially made to cut PVC pipe. It works much like scissors. I tested it and it works well, but the band saw is my hands-down favorite.

Some projects in this book require drilling into the pipe and fittings. An ordinary hand-held power drill with a normal metal or wood bit will do the job. *Note: A slow speed is recommended.*

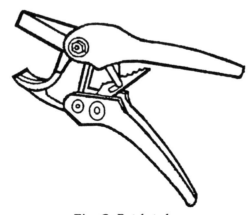

Fig. C. Ratchet shears.

Drill spade bit

Most homeowners have a drill set to cut up to ³/8-inch holes. A spade bit such as the one illustrated in FIG. D is recommended for larger holes and is a relatively inexpensive purchase. A circle cutter also can be used and is often called for in the project instructions. *Caution:* Always use a circle cutter in a drill press at a slow speed.

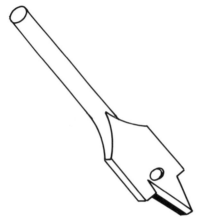

Fig. D. Drill spade bit.

To secure a joint with screws instead of cement, put at least two screws at each connection. You should use self-tapping sheet-metal screws that are plated to resist corrosion and rust. The screw should be long enough to go through both the fitting and the pipe thickness. To insert each screw, assemble the pipe and fitting and drill a hole through both pieces that is slightly smaller in diameter than the screw shank. Disassemble the pipe and fitting and enlarge the hole in the fitting only to the size of the screw shank. Reassemble the pieces and insert the screws, being careful not to tighten the screw so tight as to strip the self-cut threads in the pipe.

For your outdoor furniture, you will need to drill small (¹/4-inch) drain holes at the lowest points of your project to prevent condensation build-up. Drill into the underside of any fitting that touches the ground.

Please take special note: While I have specified the diameter of pipe holes to be cut, you might find that the specified diameters are not correct. Why, you ask? It is because while the internal diameter of the pipe is usually correct, the external diameter is not. Some pipe has thicker or thinner walls. As a result, it is always wise to measure the exterior diameter of the pipe in order to determine the true size of the hole to be drilled or cut. In some cases you might have to drill the hole and then enlarge it with a file or rasp to fit the pipe you bought. Why don't these manufacturers get together and standardize? It is because they are not in the PVC pipe furniture business.

Bending PVC pipe

PVC pipe can be bent to some extent if so desired. Bending is best accomplished by placing the pipe near a heat box containing several heat lamps until it softens, although I have had mixed results with this technique. The smaller pipe, i.e., 1-inch, can be bent by using a high-wattage hair dryer; however, this method takes forever. Another technique is to put hot sand into the pipe and let it set until the pipe can be bent. On the whole, bending PVC pipe is not a recommended procedure since the results will be mixed at best, and maintaining continuity or uniformity is difficult. None of these projects require you to bend the pipe.

Finishing your PVC project

PVC pipe is easy to paint. The bad news is, most paints won't stay on its surface, and they scratch and mar quite easily. The problem is that the pipe surface is too smooth and needs to be roughened or broken down in some way and then primed, so the paint can cling to something.

The first step in this process is to clean the pipe with a solvent that also removes the manufacturer's marks. A paint thinner with methyl ethyl ketone (MEK) is needed to do this job properly. Acetone will also work but is slower. Some paint thinners contain a combination of the chemicals that will also do the job. Wear rubber gloves and work outside with plenty of ventilation, as the fumes from MEK are toxic.

The next step is a bit tedious. Using a 120-grade sandpaper, sand all pipe and fitting surfaces. A flap-wheel sander mounted in an electric drill will speed up this process.

I suggest you do this after you have dry-assembled the project so you won't sand off the identifying labels you've marked on the various pieces. This way you can remove and sand each piece of the structure and put it back in its proper location before going on to the next piece.

If you plan to experiment with dyes or stains, do so before the assembly, and do not prime the pipe. I experimented with dyes and found out that ordinary clothing dye, the kind you buy at the grocery store, will work. The results can be varied, depending on how well you sanded the surface of the pipe and fittings. Allow the pipe and fittings to soak in the dye for at least 24 hours to get the best results.

The next step is to coat the pipe and fittings with a primer that etches the surface. You will have to check with your local paint supplier for the right product. I used a product called U-Prime that is sold by Porter Paints, a Midwest regional paint company, and it did an excellent job, but we also found primer available in hardware stores where PVC is sold.

The next step in this process is to select a paint. Here you have many options of colors and paints to use for finishing the project. Choose an oil-based paint if you want durability, but remember that oil paints are affected by ultraviolet light. Choose acrylic paint if longevity is your desire. A bright decorator varnish of mauve or blue or whatever color happens to be popular when you read this book will allow you to create very attractive and unusual furnishings for your home, both inside and out. A wood-grain stain can also be used, provided you use a white prime coat.

Developing your own designs

Once you have been bitten by the PVC bug, you will almost certainly want to experiment with your own designs. Keep in mind some simple rules: First, start with a diagram so you know the design will work. Next, don't forget to provide for the fitting allowance, the amount of pipe hidden inside the fitting. Last but not least is the assembly process. Avoid situations such as the one shown on the left in FIG. E.

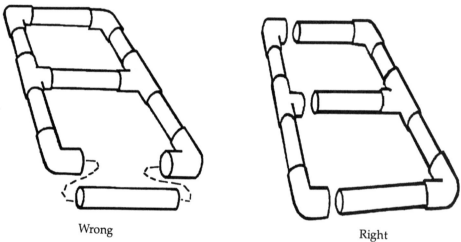

Wrong

Right

Fig. E. The wrong and right ways to assemble the pipes.

I used replacement lawn furniture cushions for most of the projects in this book, and made some of the smaller ones.

Now that I have covered the nitty-gritty, let's go build some projects and have some fun.

1
Desk caddy

Take some odds and ends of PVC pipe, paint them, add them to a piece of oak, and, voilá, you have a handsome desk caddy to hold all your pencils, paper clips, rulers, scissors, and other desk paraphernalia.

Materials

- 2 pieces 3/4-inch PVC pipe, 4 and 5 inches long
- 2 pieces 1 1/2-inch PVC pipe, 6 and 7 inches long
- 2 pieces 2-inch PVC pipe, 3 inches long
- 1 piece 2-inch PVC pipe, 5 inches long
- 1 piece 3/4-inch red oak, 8 by 14 inches

Hardware and miscellaneous

- PVC cleaner
- Epoxy glue, two-part
- Paint, yellow, oil-based (or the color of your choice)
- PVC cement
- Danish oil stain, walnut (or the finish of your choice)

Tools required

- Handheld saw
- Wood vice
- Sandpaper block
- Small paintbrush

Instructions

1. Measure, cut, and label all the pipe pieces to size. Cut one end at a 45-degree angle on all pieces as shown in FIG. 1-1, except the 5-inch length of 2-inch pipe. Cut that piece in half length-wise to form two troughs.

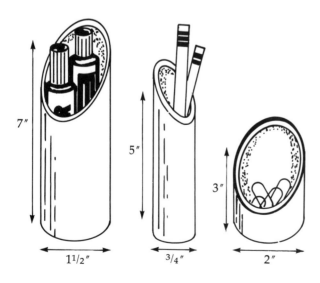

Fig. 1-1. Measure, cut, and label all pipe pieces to size.

2. Clean all marks from the pipe pieces, and sand the surfaces to roughen the finish.
3. Sand the outside bottom center of the two split pieces of 2-inch pipe, making flat spots where the two pieces can fit flush against each other. Using the cement, coat both flat surfaces and slowly count to ten, then press the two pieces together forming a C and a reverse C shape as shown in FIG. 1-2.

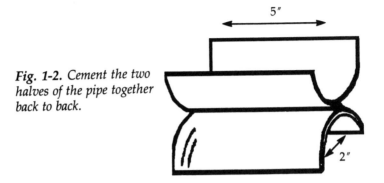

Fig. 1-2. Cement the two halves of the pipe together back to back.

4. Paint the pipe; two coats are recommended.
5. Measure and cut the red oak to size for the base. See FIG. 1-3. Sand the surface.

Fig. 1-3. Measure and cut the red oak to size for the base.

6. Stain the red oak board and allow to dry thoroughly.
7. Position the pipe pieces on the red oak board and glue. Allow to dry thoroughly before using.

2

Jenny Wren birdhouse

This project will make the bird population in your back-yard very happy. This birdhouse can be made in an after-noon with the help of your children and some scrap 4-inch PVC pipe and plywood. If you opt to add decora-tive tole painting, you can use this item inside as an accent piece.

Materials

- 1 piece 4-inch PVC pipe, 6 inches long
- 3/4-inch plywood scraps:
  - 2 pieces, 6-inch diameter, top and base
  - 2 pieces, 4-inch diameter, top and bottom plugs
  - 1 piece, 5-inch diameter, top
  - 1 piece, 1¹/2-inch PVC pipe, ³/4 inch long

Hardware and miscellaneous

- PVC cleaner
- PVC cement
- 4 weatherproofed screws, ³/4 inch
- 4 screws, 1¹/4 inch
- Epoxy glue
- Small can paint, oil-based
- 1 screw eye, #108

Tools required

- Handheld saw
- Sandpaper
- Saber saw
- Drill with countersink and 1¹/4-inch spade bits
- Screwdriver
- Small paintbrush

Instructions

House

1. Measure and cut a 6-inch length of 4-inch pipe for the body of the house. Remove markings with cleaner, and sand the surface to roughen it.
2. Measure and cut a ³/4-inch length of 1¹/2-inch pipe. Split the piece in half lengthwise. Discard one half and sand the other. This half will be the perch.
3. Center and drill a 1¹/4-inch hole into the body of the house to create a wren-sized entry.
4. Cement the perch onto the house at the bottom of the door hole as illustrated in FIG. 2-1.

Roof and floor

5. Measure and cut the pieces of ³/4-inch plywood to size using a saber saw. See FIG. 2-2.
6. Using the countersink bit, drill two holes at each end of the house, opposite one another and ³/8 inch from the edge. Figure 2-3 shows detail of placement.

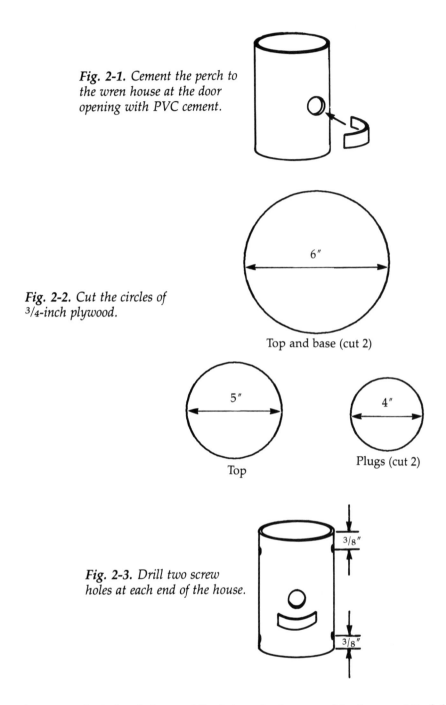

Fig. 2-1. Cement the perch to the wren house at the door opening with PVC cement.

Fig. 2-2. Cut the circles of 3/4-inch plywood.

6"

Top and base (cut 2)

5"

Top

4"

Plugs (cut 2)

Fig. 2-3. Drill two screw holes at each end of the house.

3/8"

3/8"

7. Plug a 4-inch circle of plywood flush into the bottom of the house. Attach by using 3/4-inch screws through the holes drilled in step 6. See FIG. 2-4.
8. Sand the remaining three circles of plywood, slightly rounding the edges.
9. Attach the 4-inch top plug to the 5- and 6-inch top circles as shown in FIG. 2-5

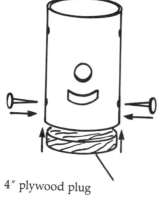

Fig. 2-4. Secure the base of the house to the pipe with ³/₄-inch screws.

4" plywood plug

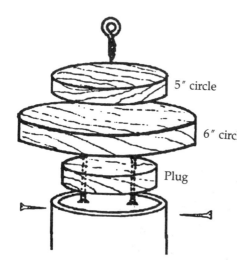

5" circle

6" circle

Plug

Fig. 2-5. Attach the 4-inch top plug to the 5-inch and 6-inch top circles before inserting it into the pipe.

using 1¹/₄-inch screws and glue. Insert this top assembly so the plug is flush into the top of the house, and attach with ³/₄-inch screws.

10. Join the base circle to the birdhouse assembly using 1¹/₄-inch screws and glue.

11. Paint the project the color of your choice.

12. Attach the screw eye in the center of the top, and hang your birdhouse so Jenny Wren can turn it into a home.

3

Six-station bird feeder

This feeder is a weekend workshop project you can do with your children and spouse as a team effort. It consists of scrap plywood and a length of 2-inch PVC pipe. You can paint it or leave it plain. In any event, the birds in your backyard are going to love it.

Materials

- 1 piece 2-inch PVC pipe, 31 inches long
- $3/4$-inch plywood exterior-grade scraps:
  1 piece, 11-inch diameter, top
  2 pieces, 8-inch diameter, center
  1 piece, 12-inch diameter, bottom
  2 pieces, 2-inch diameter, top and bottom plugs
- 2-×-4 or 2-×-6 plywood scraps:
  1 piece, $1^1/2 \times 4^1/2$ inches, lid
  1 piece, $1/8 \times 1^1/2$ inches $\times 36^1/2$ inches, bottom rim

Hardware and miscellaneous

- 8 Dacrotized screws, $3/4$ inch
- 6 screws, $1^1/4$ inch
- 12 wire brads, $1/2$ inch
- Epoxy glue
- 2 screw eyes, #108
- Paint, oil-based

Tools required

- Table saw or handsaw
- Saber saw
- Circle cutters, 2 inch and $2^3/8$ inch
- Drill with countersink and $3/4$-inch bit
- Sandpaper
- Screwdriver
- Hammer
- Small paintbrush

Instructions

Bird feeder

1. Measure and cut the 2-inch pipe to length. The suggested length is 31 inches, but you can make it as long or short as you wish. Longer is better, since it will hold more bird seed and require less frequent filling.
2. Measure and cut the $3/4$-inch plywood circles to size as shown in FIG. 3-1.
3. Using the $2^3/8$-inch circle cutter, center and cut holes in the top and center circles.
4. Drill a $3/4$-inch hole $1^1/4$ inches from the end of the pipe. Drill another hole in the opposite side, which will be the bottom of the feeder. Drill four additional holes as shown in FIG. 3-2: two $10^1/2$ inches from the bottom and two $20^1/2$ inches from the bottom.

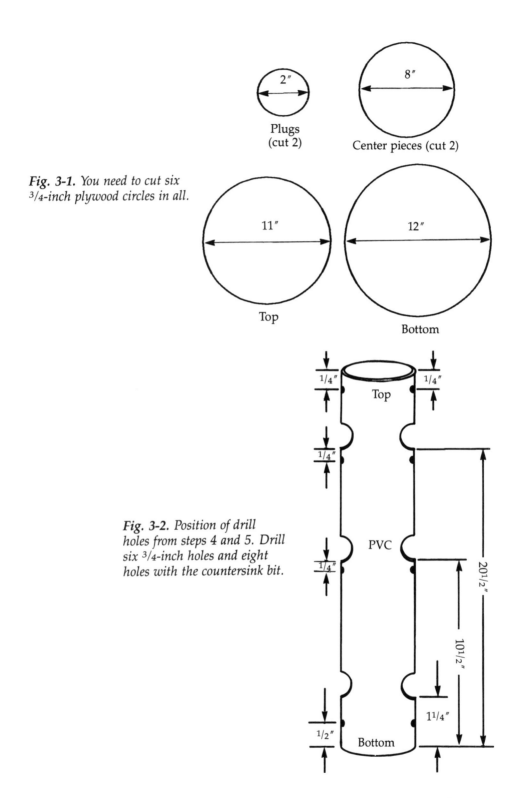

Fig. 3-1. *You need to cut six ³/₄-inch plywood circles in all.*

2″

Plugs
(cut 2)

8″

Center pieces (cut 2)

11″

Top

12″

Bottom

Fig. 3-2. *Position of drill holes from steps 4 and 5. Drill six ³/₄-inch holes and eight holes with the countersink bit.*

1/4″   Top   1/4″

1/4″

1/4″

PVC

1/2″   Bottom

20¹/₂″

10¹/₂″

1¹/₄″

5. Using the countersink bit, drill two holes 1/2 inch from the bottom underneath the 3/4-inch holes. Drill two holes 1/4 inch down from the inside bottom of the other 3/4-inch holes and 1/4 inch down from the inside of the top of the pipe (FIG. 3-2).

6. Sand the top, middle, and bottom circles thoroughly.

7. Attach the bottom circle to a 2-inch wood plug, centering it and using a 1 1/4-inch screw and glue.

8. Insert the 2-inch wood plug into the bottom of the PVC tube and secure in place with 3/4-inch screws.

9. Measure and cut the 1/8-inch wood bottom rim, and attach to the bottom circle using wire brads and glue.

10. Position the middle circles so they are flush with the bottom of the 3/4-inch holes. Position the top circle so it is flush with the top of the pipe. Hold all circles in place with glue and two 3/4-inch wood screws inserted through the inside of the PVC tube.

11. Measure and cut the lid from 2-×-6 stock. Sand the rough edges.

12. Center and attach the 2-inch wood plug to the lid and hold in place with a 1 1/4-inch screw.

13. Attach the two screw eyes at opposite points on the 11-inch top circle. Put the lid in place. You might have to sand the plug slightly to get a snug fit.

14. Sand the exposed pipe to roughen the surface. Paint the project the color of your choice.

15. Fill the feeder with bird seed, and go hang it from your back porch or a tree limb. Stand back and watch the birds, and probably squirrels, enjoy the welcome addition to your yard.

4

Umbrella stand

This project is a welcome addition to any home or office entrance. You can decorate it with wallpaper, stencil it, or just leave it plain. This fairly simple project can be made in less than an hour.

Materials

- 1 piece 4-inch PVC pipe, 20 inches long
- 2-inch red oak:
  1 piece, 7-inch diameter, bottom
  1 piece, 6-inch diameter, top

Hardware and miscellaneous

- PVC cleaner
- Epoxy glue
- Paint, oil-based

Tools required

- Handsaw
- Sandpaper
- Circle cutter (4- to 5-inch capability)
- Drill press
- Drill with 1/4-inch bit
- Saber saw
- Small paintbrush

Instructions

1. Measure and cut the 4-inch pipe to length. Make certain you have perfect 90-degree cuts at both ends.
2. Clean all marks from the pipe, and sand the surface thoroughly to roughen it.
3. Measure and cut the 6- and 7-inch circles from the 2-inch red oak (actual thickness 1½ inch).
4. Using a circle cutter and a drill press, cut a dado the width of the pipe wall to a depth of approximately 1 inch into the bottom and top circles (FIG. 4-1).

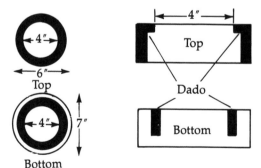

Fig. 4-1. Cut a dado to fit the pipe in the top and bottom circles. Then cut a 4-inch diameter circle from the top piece.

5. Drill a starter hole into the top circle, and cut out the 4-inch center using a saber saw (FIG. 4-1 top left).
6. Sand the bottom and top circles thoroughly, rounding the inside and outside edges.
7. Drill four 1/4-inch holes 1/2 inch from the top and bottom of the pipe at opposite sides as illustrated in FIG. 4-2. These holes will help the glue keep the top and bottom circles in place.

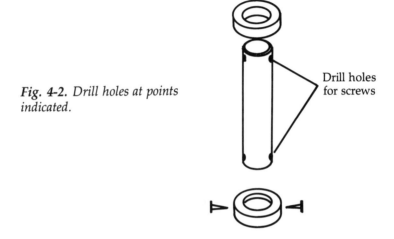

Fig. 4-2. Drill holes at points indicated.

Drill holes for screws

8. Glue the top and bottom pieces to the pipe. Allow to dry thoroughly.
9. Decorate your project to fit the decor of your home, and fill it with all of your umbrellas, canes, and other items you want to keep handy.

5

Chaise lounge and table

This project is going to provide the most used pieces of furniture that ever decorated your patio, deck, or yard. Comfortable and durable are the two words that best describe this attractive chaise lounge and table set. Both use standard PVC pressure pipe fittings and can be constructed easily in an afternoon.

Materials

Chaise

- 1$\frac{1}{2}$-inch PVC pipe, 35 feet long ($\frac{7}{8}$-inch fitting allowance), cut to size as follows:

  6 pieces 11$\frac{1}{2}$ inches long (P1)
  6 pieces 5 inches long (P2)
  2 pieces 21$\frac{1}{4}$ inches long (P3)
  2 pieces 18 inches long (P4)
  2 pieces 15 inches long (P5)
  2 pieces 12 inches long (P6)
  2 pieces 7 inches long (P7)
  2 pieces 12$\frac{1}{4}$ inches long (P8)
  2 pieces 6$\frac{1}{2}$ inches long (P9)
  2 pieces 10$\frac{1}{2}$ inches long (P10)
  4 pieces 20 inches long (P11)
  14 pieces 1$\frac{3}{4}$ inches long (P12)

- 1$\frac{1}{2}$-inch PVC fittings:

  12 elbows, 90 degrees
  24 tees

Table

- 1$\frac{1}{2}$-inch PVC pipe, 15 feet long ($\frac{7}{8}$-inch fitting allowance), cut to size as follows:

  8 pieces 10 inches long (T1)
  6 pieces 15 inches long (T2)

- 1$\frac{1}{2}$-inch PVC fittings:

  8 elbows, 90 degrees
  4 tees

- 2 pieces $\frac{1}{4}$-inch glass:

  1 piece 14 $\times$ 22 inches
  1 piece 15 $\times$ 15 inches

Hardware and miscellaneous

- 1 piece canvas sling, 20 $\times$ 80 inches
- Matching heavy-duty thread
- 1 standard chaise cushion, 70 inches long
- 1 pint PVC cement
- 1 pint primer
- 1 pint paint, fuchsia (or the color of your choice)
- 10 sheet-metal screws 1 inch

Tools required

- Handsaw
- Screwdriver
- Sandpaper or flap sander
- Drill with $1/16$-inch bit
- Rubber mallet
- Sewing machine
- Paint brush

Instructions

Chaise

The frame consists of two sides, a back and four pieces of pipe that join the two sides. I suggest you assemble the whole unit before cementing the joints. Make certain the unit is aligned and flat to the ground so it has no rocking motion. Cement each side first, then the back, and finally, the back and center pieces to the sides. You might wish to use sheet-metal screws to attach the center pieces, so that the unit can be taken apart for storage.

1. Measure, cut, and label the lengths of straight pipe.
2. Begin the side assembly by joining its back pieces first, including the arm rests and the base section (FIG. 5-1). Add the front section. Use the P12 pieces to join all fittings shown next to each other. Make certain to leave no gap between those fittings.

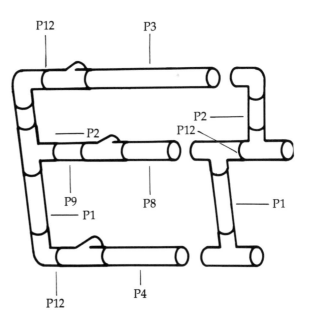

Fig. 5-1. Assemble the first side with the pieces shown. Note: P12 pieces are not shown in this illustration; insert them where indicated.

3. Make a mirror image of the first side, as shown in FIG. 5-2, and turn all open fittings so they face inward.

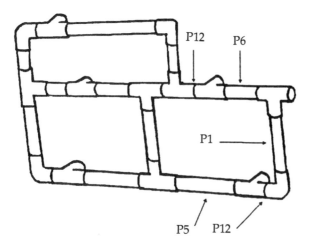

Fig. 5-2. Make a mirror image of the first side, turning all open fittings so they face inward. Note: P12 pieces are not shown in this illustration; insert them where indicated.

4. Assemble the back section as shown in FIG. 5-3.

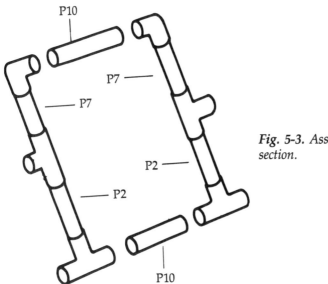

Fig. 5-3. Assemble the back section.

5. Attach the back assembly to the sides, using the P10 and P11 pipe for this purpose. Make certain no gaps are between the back and side fittings. See FIG. 5-4.
6. Using a rubber mallet, tap all of the pipe and fittings to ensure a snug fit.
7. At this point, you may have to adjust the length of some of the pipe so the chaise pieces all fit together properly and do not have any rocking motion. The chaise must sit firmly on the ground at both the front and back.

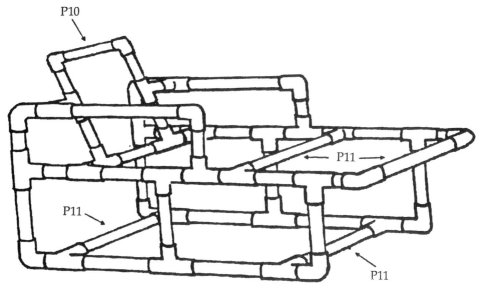

Fig. 5-4. *Attach the back assembly to the sides.*

8. Using the rubber mallet, gently knock the back side pieces apart. Keep the fittings at the proper angle at all times. Begin cementing pieces together. Remember, you only have a few seconds before the bond is set and you cannot move the connection. This point is extremely crucial in the assembly. Move your way forward until all the sides pieces have been fused together.

9. Remove the back assembly and lay it on a very flat workbench or table surface. Cement the pieces together. Make certain the fittings are flat against the working surface.

10. Reattach the back to the side assemblies, and once again verify that the chaise bottom is flat on the ground and does not rock.

11. At this point, you can either cement the remaining pieces together, or you can fasten them with sheet-metal screws for later disassembly. However, before you decide, make the sling that will fit over and around the center pieces and back.

Sling

Make the sling from any heavy canvas material. You can make it yourself or find a friend who owns a sewing machine. If you wish, you can also substitute the sling with a piece of 1/4-inch exterior-grade plywood for the base and back. Simply make it slightly narrower than the cushion you plan to use.

The sling should be hemmed at the sides and have loops of about 7 inches of material to fit around the top and bottom pipe at the back, and around the center and front pipe of the seat area. The sling should have very little slack. See FIG. 5-5.

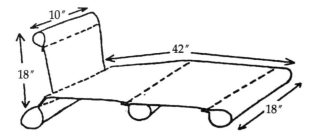

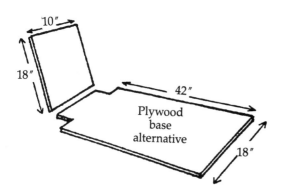

Fig. 5-5. *Make a canvas sling or plywood base to the dimensions shown.*

12. Before beginning the final assembly, clean the pipe and fittings to remove all of the markings. If you plan to paint the project, roughen the pipe and fittings with sandpaper or a flap-wheel sander mounted in a drill.
13. Paint the project with the primer and allow the paint to dry thoroughly. Finish with the color of your choice. Two coats are advised, with a short drying period between coats.
14. Attach the sling to the chaise and cement or fasten the center and back pieces. If you don't use cement, put at least two sheet-metal screws at opposite sides of each joint. Predrill a ¹/₁₆-inch hole in each fitting-and-pipe joint and insert the screws, being careful to not overtighten them.
15. You can make a cushion for the chaise, or you can buy a standard replacement cushion from most discount or home centers.

Table

16. Measure and cut the PVC pipe for the table.
17. Dry-assemble all of the pieces on a flat surface as illustrated in FIG. 5-6.
18. Disassemble and reassemble all pieces using PVC pipe cement.
19. I used precut glass inserts for the top and center. The size is 14×22 inches for the top and 15×15 inches for the center piece. You might opt to make yours

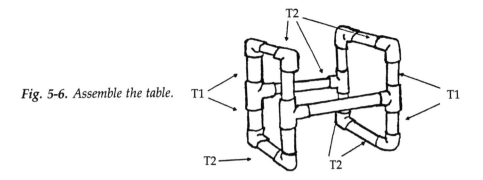

Fig. 5-6. Assemble the table.

out of plywood. If so, make certain you use an exterior-grade 3/4-inch ply-wood, and seal and paint the surface.

20. Sit back and admire your finished project.

6
Octagonal patio table

This attractive and functional piece of furniture would look just as good indoors or outdoors. You can cover it with a glass top or create a designer top of wood to match your other furniture. This project can be completed quickly; it is guaranteed to make you proud of your efforts.

Materials

- 1-inch PVC pipe, 10 feet long, cut to size as follows:
  8 pieces 8 inches long (P1)
  16 pieces 3$1/4$ inches long (P2)
  4 pieces 14 inches long (P3)
- 1-inch PVC fittings:
  16 elbows, 45 degrees
  8 tees
- 1 piece $1/2$-inch glass, beveled, 36-inch diameter, octagonal-shaped

Hardware and miscellaneous

- PVC cement
- PVC cleaner
- 16 small self-adhesive foam rubber or felt pads

Tools required

- Handsaw
- Rubber mallet
- Sandpaper

Instructions

Table frame

1. Measure, cut, and label the lengths of straight pipe as listed.
2. Working on a flat surface, assemble the top and bottom frames. Make certain the two assemblies are mirror images. See FIG. 6-1.

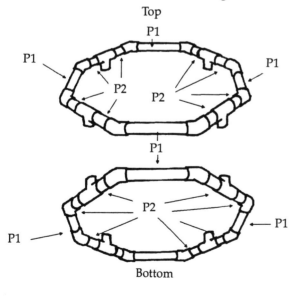

Top
P1
P1
P1
P1
P2
P2
P1

Fig. 6-1. The top and bottom frames should be mirror images of one another.

P1
P2
P1
P1

Bottom

3. Using the 14-inch pieces labeled P3, connect the top and bottom frames as shown in FIG. 6-2. Use a rubber mallet to ensure all pipe and fittings are snug. Make any necessary corrections to pipe length, so the unit is a perfect octagonal shape with the top and bottom identical.

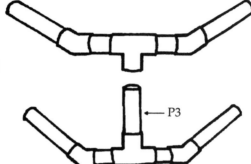

Fig. 6-2. Connect the top and bottom frames with P3 pipes.

4. With the bottom on a flat surface, pull apart the bottom pieces and reassemble one piece at a time with cement. Turn the structure over, and do the same to the top. Cement the 14-inch pieces to the top and bottom last.
5. Remove any markings from the PVC pipe and fittings with cleaner. If you plan to paint this project, sand the surface to roughen it.

Tabletop

6. You can make a wood top for this table or purchase a glass top. If you use glass, be certain to also purchase at least 16 small self-stick pads for the top of each of the PVC fittings to cushion the glass and keep it from slipping off. See FIG. 6-3.
7. Go pick your favorite spot and show off your new table.

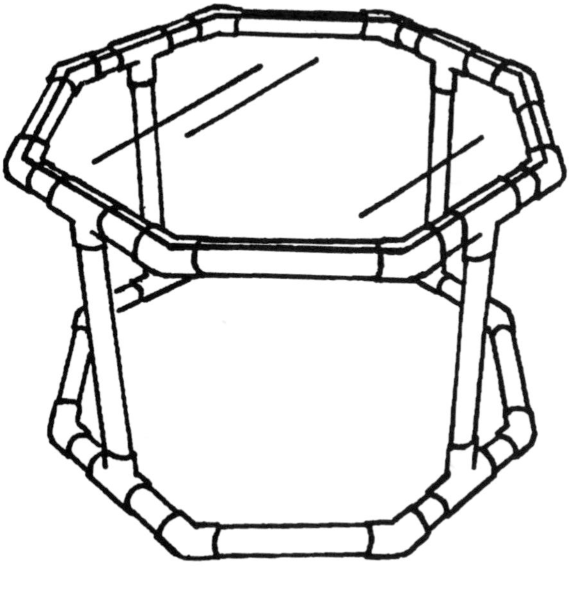

Fig. 6-3. Use self-adhesive pads to secure the tabletop.

7

Patio sofa and chair with table

This ensemble will look good in the family room, on the patio, or around the pool. Straightforward and simple construction make each of these designs easy weekend workshop projects to tackle. The chair and the sofa use standard cushions found at most home centers and discount houses.

Materials

Chair

- $1^1/2$-inch PVC pipe, 20 feet long ($^7/8$-inch fitting allowance), cut to size as follows:
  6 pieces $5^1/4$ inches long (C1)
  4 pieces 7 inches long (C2)
  4 pieces 11 inches long (C3)
  2 pieces 17 inches long (C4)
  2 pieces $1^1/4$ inches long (C5)
  4 pieces 22 inches long (C6)
- $1^1/2$-inch fittings:
  8 elbows, 90 degrees
  2 elbows, 45 degrees
  8 tees

Sofa

- $1^1/2$-inch PVC pipe, 31 feet long ($^7/8$-inch fitting allowance), cut to size as follows:
  4 pieces 9 inches long (S1)
  6 pieces $20^1/2$ inches long (S2)
  6 pieces $11^1/2$ inches long (S3)
  8 pieces 18 inches long (S4)
  1 piece 47 inches long (S5)
  12 pieces $1^3/4$ inches long (S6)
- $1^1/2$-inch fittings:
  8 elbows, 90 degrees
  2 elbows, 45 degrees
  18 tees

Table

- $1^1/2$-inch PVC pipe, 11 feet long ($^7/8$-inch fitting allowance), cut to size as follows:
  2 pieces 11 inches long (T1)
  4 pieces 5 inches long (T2)
  2 pieces 15 inches long (T3)
  4 pieces $12^1/2$ inches long (T4)
- $1^1/2$-inch fittings:
  4 elbows, 90 degrees
  4 tees
  4 end caps

Hardware and miscellaneous

- PVC cleaner
- PVC cement
- Sheet-metal screws
- 4 yards heavy-duty canvas
- Matching heavy-duty thread
- 1 piece plywood, $3/4 \times 22 \times 41$ inches
- 2 wood strips, $3/4 \times 42^{1}/_{2}$ inches
- 2 wood strips, $3/4 \times 22$ inches
- Clear silicone or epoxy glue
- 10 finishing nails, $1^{1}/_{2}$ inch
- Seat cushions

Tools required

- Handsaw
- Sandpaper
- Rubber mallet
- Drill with $1/_{16}$-inch bit
- Sewing machine

Instructions

Chair

1. Measure, cut, and label the pipe as listed.
2. Assemble the patio chair first. Put the side pieces together as shown in FIG. 7-1 without cementing the joints. Make certain the pipe and the fittings go together so that both sides of the chair are mirror images and sit firmly on the ground.

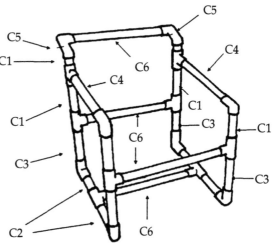

Fig. 7-1. Assemble the patio chair as shown. Note: C5 pieces are not shown in this illustration; insert them where indicated.

3. Once you are certain everything is correct, begin dismantling the chair and reassembling each side with cement.
4. If you plan to disassemble the chair for storage, use sheet-metal screws to attach the center pieces to the sides instead of cementing them.
5. Remove the marks from the pipe and fittings. If you plan to paint the pipe and fittings, sand them until the surface is dull.

Chair sling

6. Measure and cut the canvas to the size shown in FIG. 7-2. Hem the sides and sew three loops to fit over the pipe. Allow at least 7 inches for the loops. The sling must fit tightly with no sagging.

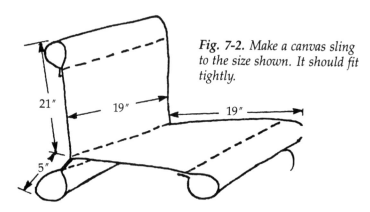

Fig. 7-2. Make a canvas sling to the size shown. It should fit tightly.

7. Attach the sling to the center pieces and fasten the center pieces to the chair sides using cement or sheet-metal screws (FIG. 7-3).

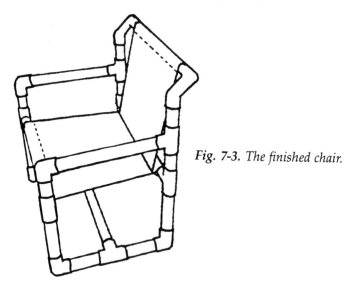

Fig. 7-3. The finished chair.

Sofa

8. Assemble the sofa pieces as shown in FIG. 7-4. Again, dry-assemble and double-check the fittings and pipe to ensure the sizes are correct and that the sofa sits firmly on the ground. Make certain you do this on a flat floor or concrete slab.

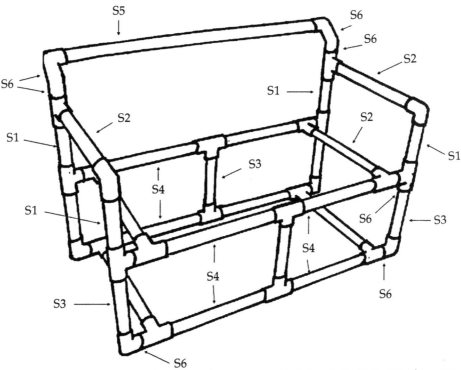

Fig. 7-4. *Assemble the sofa the same way you assembled the chair. Note: S6 pieces are not shown in this illustration; insert them where indicated.*

Sofa slings

9. Measure and cut the canvas for the sofa slings according to FIG. 7-5. Hem the sides, and sew loops at the ends for attachment to the sofa center pieces as shown. Again, make certain the slings fit tightly, with no slack in the center.
10. Knock down and reassemble the sofa sides and connect all pieces with the center assembly. Attach the slings and then cement the sides or attach them with sheet-metal screws.

Table

11. Assemble the table as shown in FIG. 7-6. Dry-assemble all pieces and make certain the pieces fit correctly before reassembly.

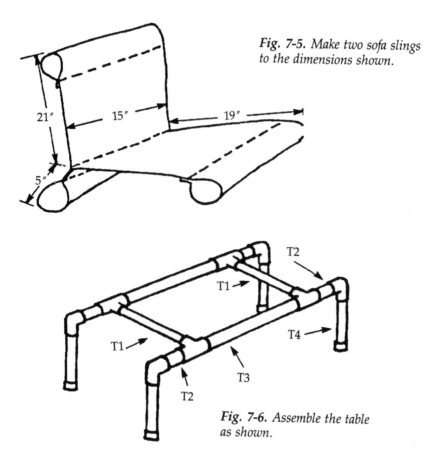

Fig. 7-5. Make two sofa slings to the dimensions shown.

21" 15" 19" 5"

T2 T1 T4 T1 T2 T3

Fig. 7-6. Assemble the table as shown.

12. Knock down the table and reassemble with cement.
13. The tabletop can be glass or wood or plastic. Allow a 4-inch overhang at all sides.
14. You can make your own cushions, or you can buy standard yard furniture replacement cushions at most discount houses and home centers.
15. Go stand back and look at the luxury you just created for your backyard.

8

Picnic in the round

This project not only looks great on a patio or deck but will be something you use over and over. The combination table and chairs provide room for lots of hungry friends. And you won't have to worry about baking in the hot sun, since the table supports a standard umbrella.

Materials

Chair

- $1\frac{1}{2}$-inch PVC pipe, 20 feet per chair (1-inch fitting allowance), cut to size as follows:
  4 pieces $21\frac{1}{2}$ (C1)
  2 pieces $17\frac{3}{4}$ inches long (C2)
  4 pieces $1\frac{1}{2}$ inches long (C3)
  4 pieces $7\frac{3}{4}$ inches long (C4)
  6 pieces $5\frac{3}{4}$ inches long (C5)
  2 pieces 2 inches long (C6)
- $1\frac{1}{2}$-inch fittings per chair (Note: use only pressure-type fittings for this project):
  10 elbows, 90 degrees
  8 tees
- 4-×-8-foot plywood, exterior-grade, $\frac{1}{2}$ inch thick, cut to size as follows:
  1 piece $19 \times 2\frac{1}{2}$ inches, seat
  1 piece 19×17 inches, seat back
  1 piece 19×1 inches, support
- $\frac{3}{4}$-inch PVC pipe, 15 feet per chair, cut to size as follows:
  8 pieces 20 inches long (C7)

Table

- $1\frac{1}{2}$-inch PVC pipe, 21 feet (1-inch fitting allowance)
  8 pieces $20\frac{1}{2}$ inches long (T1)
  4 pieces 22 inches long (T2)
- $1\frac{1}{2}$-inch fittings
  8 elbows, 90 degrees
  2 double tees
- 4-×-4-foot plywood, exterior-grade, $\frac{3}{4}$ inch thick

Hardware and miscellaneous

- PVC cement
- PVC cleaner
- Self-tapping 1-inch sheet-metal screws
- 24 molly bolts, $\frac{7}{8}$-inch (6 per chair)
- 16 No. 6 flathead wood screws, 1-inch (4 per chair)
- Clear silicone glue
- Seat cushions
- 15 feet pine lattice, $\frac{1}{8} \times 1$ inch, tabletop trim, or rip from 3-foot length 2-×-4-foot board
- 8 No. 6 flathead wood screws, $2\frac{3}{4}$ inches long

- 3d finishing nails
- Wood stain or paint
- Polyurethane

Tools required

- Handsaw
- Sandpaper
- Rubber mallet
- Drill with $1^1/_2$-inch spade bit
- Sewing machine
- Table saw
- Jigsaw
- Drill press
- Rasp
- Screwdriver
- Paintbrush

Instructions

Chairs

1. Measure, cut, and label the pipe as listed.
2. Assemble a chair first. Put the pieces together as shown in FIG. 8-1 without cementing the joints. Make certain the pipe and the fittings go together so both sides of the chair are mirror images and fit firmly on the ground.

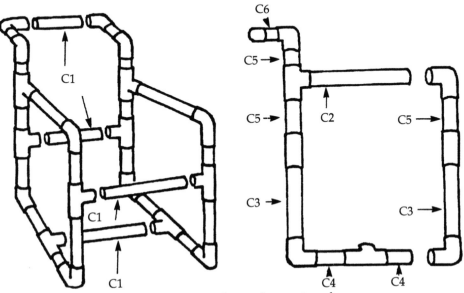

Fig. 8-1. Assemble the sides of the chair first and connect as shown.

3. Once you are certain everything is correct, begin dismantling the chair and reassembling each side with cement.

4. If you plan to disassemble the chair for storage, use sheet-metal screws to attach the crossbars to the sides instead of cementing them.

5. To shape the vertical C7 bars so they fit inside the chair frame sides, wrap a 1 1/2-inch scrap piece of PVC with sandpaper and mount this piece in a drill press. Round a 1/8-inch well into the C7 pipe ends with a rasp, and finish shaping by sanding against the wrapped pipe.

6. Check for fit in the chair frame. Be careful not to sand too much, or these vertical bars will fit too loosely. Cement four vertical bars in each side of the chair frame.

7. Assemble the remaining chairs in the same manner. Again, dry-assemble and double-check to ensure the sizes are correct and the chair sits firmly on the floor.

8. Using cleaner, remove all marks from the pipe and fittings. If you plan to paint the pipe and fittings, sand them until the surface is dull.

9. Measure and cut the 1/2-inch plywood to the sizes for the seat pieces, and stain or paint.

10. Attach the plywood seat pieces to the crossbars with molly bolts and to the support strips with glue and the 1-inch wood screws. See FIG. 8-2.

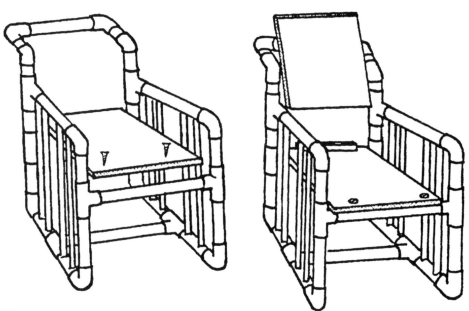

Fig. 8-2. Attaching the seat pieces.

Table

11. Dry-assemble the table as shown in FIG. 8-3. Make certain the pieces fit correctly before reassembly.

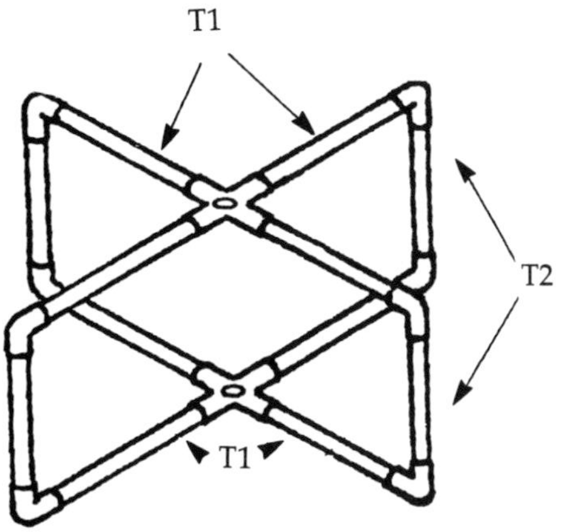

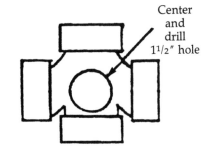

T1

T2

Fig. 8-3. *Assemble the table frame as shown.*

T1

12. Mark the centers of the two double tees.
13. Disassemble the table frame and cut a hole in each of the double tees, large enough to fit your umbrella pole. The hole should be cut through both sides of the upper double tee and through the top side only of the base double tee. See FIG. 8-4.

Fig. 8-4. *Cut holes in the centers of the double tees to fit the umbrella pole.*

Center
and
drill
1¹/₂″ hole

14. Reassemble the table frame with cement.
15. Make the tabletop from the 4- × -4-foot plywood, rounding the corners with a jigsaw and cutting a hole in the center in line with the double tees' umbrella holes. Attach the pine strips around the outside with glue and finishing nails as illustrated in FIG. 8-5. We stained it a driftwood color and coated it with polyurethane.

Fig. 8-5. *Finish the tabletop by running pine strips around the outside edge.*

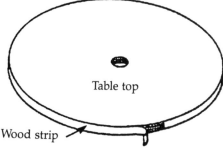

Table top

Wood strip

16. Attach the tabletop to the frame from the underside with two 2³/₄-inch wood screws at each connection point, through the PVC and into the wood. Drill small starter holes through the PVC pipe to make this process easier.
17. You can make your own cushions if you are handy, or you can buy standard yard furniture replacement cushions at most discount houses and home centers.
18. Put the umbrella in its new home and fire up the grill.

9

Canopy bench

This bench seats three and is something you can put any-where around or in the house. With its canopy cover, this project is certain to gain a lot of attention from all your friends and neighbors. You might want to make more than one, since you might wind up taking orders.

Materials

Canopy

- $1^1/2$-inch PVC pipe, 24 feet long ($^3/4$-inch fitting allowance), cut to size as follows:
  2 pieces 38 inches long (C1)
  4 pieces $3^3/4$ inches long (C2)
  2 pieces $33^1/2$ inches long (C3)
  2 pieces 44 inches long (C4)
  2 pieces 19 inches long (C5)
- $1^1/2$-inch fittings
  4 elbows, 90 degrees
  4 tees

Seating area

- $1^1/2$-inch PVC pipe, 35 feet long ($^3/4$-inch fitting allowance), cut to size as follows:
  1 piece 50 inches long (S1)
  4 pieces 24 inches long (S2)
  7 pieces 19 inches long (S3)
  6 pieces $12^1/2$ inches long (S4)
  4 pieces $10^1/2$ inches long (S5)
  2 pieces 8 inches long (S6)
- $^3/4$-inch PVC pipe, 32 feet long, cut to size as follows:
  10 pieces $13^1/2$ inches long (S7)
  10 pieces 24 inches long (S8)
- $1^1/2$-inch fittings:
  6 elbows, 90 degrees
  12 tees

Hardware and miscellaneous

- PVC cement
- PVC cleaner
- 6 wood strips, $^3/4 \times 12$ inches
- 1 piece plywood, $^5/8 \times 19 \times 50$ inches
- 1 piece canvas, 32×64 inches
- 1 length fringe, 150 inches
- 20 screws, Dacrotized, $1^1/2$ inches
- Seat and back cushions

Tools required

- Handsaw
- Rubber mallet

- Sandpaper
- Drill press with 1-inch bit and circle cutter and 1-inch sanding drum
- Drill with flap sander

Instructions

Bench

1. Measure, cut, and label the straight pipe to size. Sand any burns off the ends of each pipe piece. Figure 9-1 shows the full assembly of all these pieces.

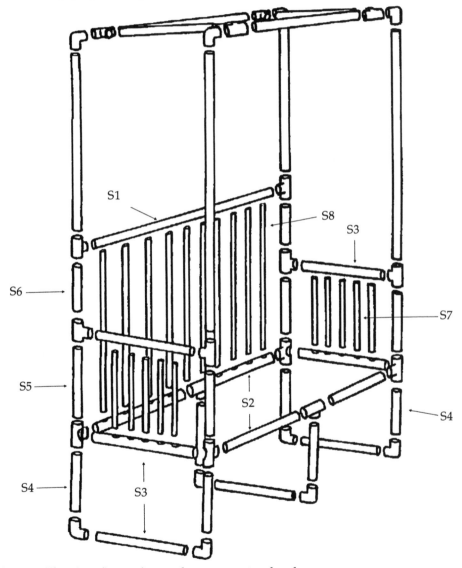

Fig. 9-1. The pipes fit together as shown to create a bench.

2. Take two of the pieces labeled S2 and the one marked S1. Measure the positions for drilling 1-inch holes to hold the S8 pipes by finding the center of the S1 pipe and then measuring 2½ inches to either side of this center mark. Measure and mark each additional location for drilling 5 inches from these starting marks for a total of 10 locations. Mark S2, the 24-inch pipe, with the same drill positions by aligning the ends of the two S2 pipes at the ends of the S1 pipe. Make certain the holes are in a straight line. Refer to FIG. 9-2 for guidance.

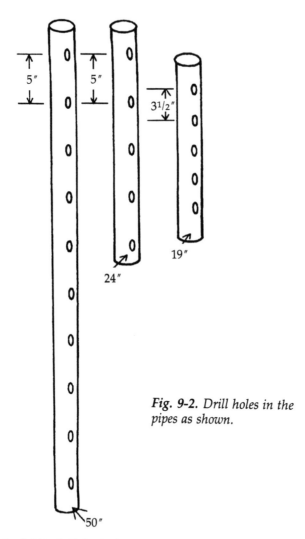

Fig. 9-2. Drill holes in the pipes as shown.

3. Using a 1-inch bit, drill the holes into the pipe from above. Depending on the actual outside thickness of the S8 pipes, it may be necessary to enlarge the holes slightly. Use a small 1-inch sanding drum inserted into a drill for this purpose.

4. Take four of the 19-inch pipe pieces labeled S3 and mark the locations for drilling the 1-inch holes to hold the 3/4-inch pipe labeled S7 that forms the side of the canopy bench. Do this by finding and marking the center of the S3 pipe and then measuring and marking 3½ inches to either side. Each successive position is 3½ inches to the left and right for a total of five locations. Again, refer to FIG. 9-2 for guidance. Make certain the holes are in a straight line on the pipe. Repeat step 3 for these pipe pieces.
5. Drill a hole large enough to fit the outer diameter of the 1½-inch pipe in the side center of four of the tee fittings. Use a drill press with a circle cutter. This size should be about 1⅞ inches. You must measure your pipe's actual outside diameter to determine this size. See FIG. 9-3.

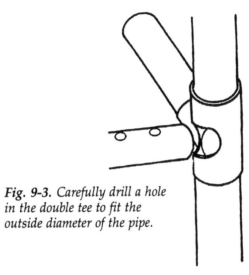

Fig. 9-3. Carefully drill a hole in the double tee to fit the outside diameter of the pipe.

6. Assemble the pipe pieces and fittings needed to make the lower portion of the bench. Refer back to FIG. 9-1.
7. Begin the assembly by starting with the bottom of the bench and working upward. Dry-assembly all pieces first, working on a flat surface. The 3/4-inch pipe pieces (S7, S8) should fit snugly in the holes drilled for them. Again, refer to back to FIG. 9-1.
8. To make the seat supports, attach the 3/4-inch wood strips around the inside of the PVC frame using the 1½-inch screws. See FIG. 9-4.
9. When the supports are secure, attach the 5/8-inch plywood to them with the 1½-inch screws.
10. Assemble the canopy top, and add it to the bench. See FIG. 9-5.
11. When you are certain all the pieces fit properly, the canopy bench sits firmly on the ground, and everything seems correct, begin cementing the pieces together, starting at the top.
12. Using the cleaner, remove all marks from the pipe. If you plan to paint it, the pipe must be sanded thoroughly to roughen the shiny surface.

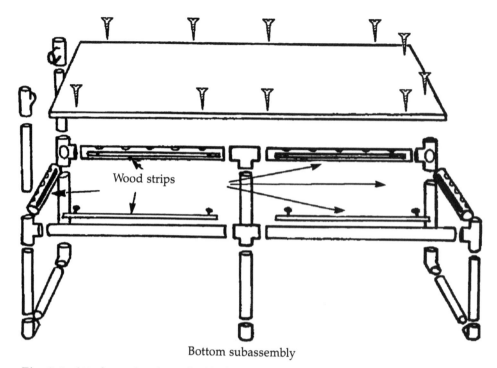

Wood strips

Bottom subassembly

Fig. 9-4. Attach wood strips to inside frame to make seat supports.

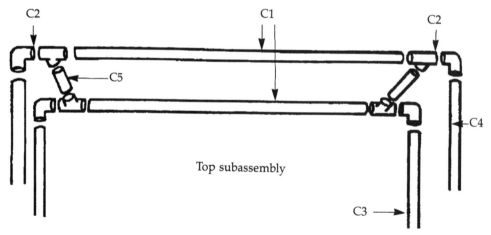

C2   C1   C2

C5

C4

Top subassembly

C3

Fig. 9-5. Assemble the canopy frame. Note: C2 pieces are not shown in this illustration; insert them where indicated.

Canopy

13. You can make the canopy from cloth or canvas. I recommend canvas if you are going to use the project outside. The cover is basically a 24- × -54-inch box

with a 4-inch overhang. The cover must fig snugly, with no sagging. I added fringe to the bottom edge of the cover for a little something extra. Let your imagination go free. You will be surprised at what you create, but don't forget to include an inch for seam allowance to each seam edge when you measure. See FIG. 9-6.

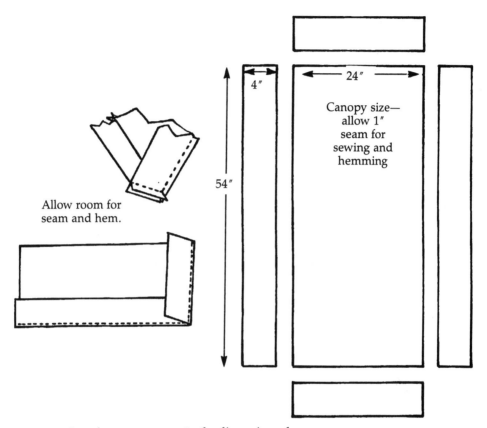

Allow room for seam and hem.

4″

54″

24″

Canopy size—allow 1″ seam for sewing and hemming

Fig. 9-6. Sew the canopy cover to the dimensions shown.

14. Standard yard furniture replacement cushions will fit this project for both the seat and back. I made extra throw pillows for an added touch.

10

Basic bookcase

This rather straightforward project can be used in every room of the house. The basic design can be modified to be used on the patio to display plants or you can use it in the kids' rooms to keep books and toys off the floor. Make the bookcase in a couple of hours in an evening, or save it for a great weekend workshop project.

Materials

- 1¹/₂-inch PVC pipe, 32 feet long (⁷/₈-inch fitting allowance), cut to size as follows:
  4 pieces 59 inches long (P1)
  4 pieces 24 inches long (P2)
  4 pieces 7¹/₂ inches long (P3)
  8 pieces 1¹/₄ inches long (P4)
- ³/₄-inch PVC pipe, 10 feet long, cut to size as follows:
  10 pieces 11 inches long (P5)
- 1¹/₂-inches fittings
  4 elbows, 90 degrees
  12 tees

Hardware and miscellaneous

- 6 pine shelves 1×8×28 inches each
- Twenty 1¹/₂-inch screws
- PVC cement
- PVC cleaner

Tools required

- Rubber mallet
- Drill with ¹/₈-inch and 1-inch bits and 1-inch sanding drum
- Handsaw
- Square
- Chalk line
- Screwdriver

Instructions

Bookcase

1. Measure, cut, and label the straight pipe pieces as listed.
2. Assemble the fittings and pipe pieces that form the bookcase bottom, referring to the diagram shown in FIG. 10-1.
3. Using a square, make certain the pieces marked P2 and P3 and their respective tees are at 90-degrees angles, or *square*, to one another.
4. Measure and mark the four 59-inch pipes labeled P1 for the five 1-inch holes to hold the ³/₄-inch pipe shelf supports, labeled P5. This step is best done with a chalk line to make a straight line on one side of each pipe. Mark the

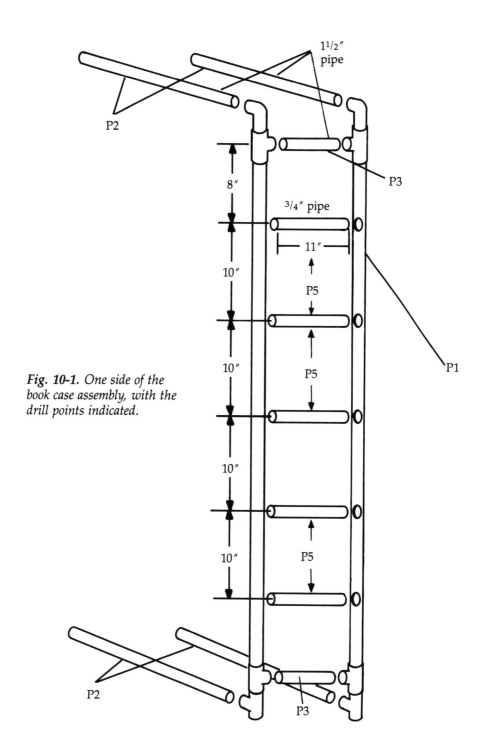

Fig. 10-1. *One side of the book case assembly, with the drill points indicated.*

drill points at 8 inches from one end and 10 inches thereafter, i.e., 18, 28, 38, and 48 inches. It is extremely important that the holes are aligned properly.

5. Drill all of the 1-inch holes into the P1 pipes. Enlarge the holes if necessary with a sanding drum inserted into a handheld drill. You can also do this with a pocketknife.

6. Insert the 3/4-inch pipe pieces into two of the P1 pipes and insert this assembly into the base of the bookcase from step 2.

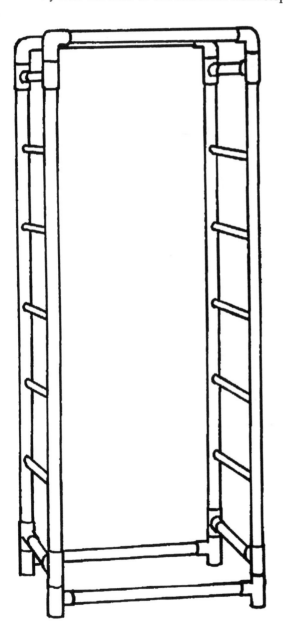

Fig. 10-2. Assembled bookshelf before shelves are in place.

7. Dry-assemble the top of the bookcase. Using a square, make certain that the P2 and P3 pipe connections are square.
8. Knock down the bookcase assembly, starting at the top, and begin cementing the fittings and pipe together. Make certain the top and bottom are square when you reassemble the fittings and pipe. Figure 10-2 shows the assembled bookshelf—minus the shelves.
9. Drill two 1/8-inch holes centered and about 5 inches apart into each of the P5 pipe shelf supports, to hold the shelves in place.

Shelves

10. Measure and cut the 1-×-8 boards to 28-inch lengths.
11. If you wish to paint the boards white to match the color of the pipe, or any color for that matter, do so now.
12. Attach each shelf to the top of the two shelf support pipes and hold in place with four 1 1/2-inch screws from the bottom as shown in FIG. 10-3.

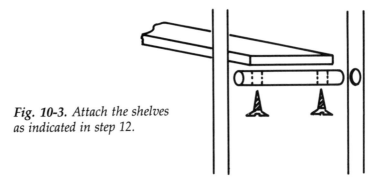

Fig. 10-3. Attach the shelves as indicated in step 12.

13. Go position your bookcase where you want it and stand back to admire your handiwork.

11
Canopy yard swing

This versatile design allows you to use the swing with or without its companion A-frame. But if you don't have a porch on your house, the A-frame lets you enjoy that special pleasure of a traditional porch swing anywhere you want to place it.

Materials

A-frame

- 2-inch PVC pipe, 70 feet long ($1^1/_8$-inch fitting allowance), cut to size as follows:
  4 pieces 72 inches long (C1)
  3 pieces $60^1/_4$ inches long (C2)
  2 pieces $50^1/_2$ inches long (C3)
  1 piece $43^1/_2$ inches long (C4)
  4 pieces $29^1/_4$ inches long (C5)
  4 pieces 8 inches long (C6)
  4 pieces $5^1/_2$ inches long (C7)
  16 pieces $2^1/_4$ inches long (C8)
- 2-inch fittings:
  16 elbows, 90 degrees
  4 elbows, 45 degrees
  12 tees

Swing

- $1^1/_2$-inch PVC pipe, 22 feet long ($1^1/_8$-inch fitting allowance), cut to size as follows:
  3 pieces $39^1/_2$ inches long (S1)
  4 pieces $19^1/_2$ inches long (S2)
  2 pieces $10^1/_2$ inches long (S3)
  4 pieces $4^3/_8$ inches long (S4)
  2 pieces $3^7/_8$ inches long (S5)
  6 pieces $2^1/_4$ inches long (S6)
- $3/_4$-inch PVC pipe, 45 feet long, cut to size as follows:
  10 pieces 25 inches long (S7)
  11 pieces 24 inches long (S8)
- $1^1/_2$-inch fittings:
  4 elbows, 90 degrees
  10 tees
  4 end caps

Hardware and miscellaneous

- PVC cement
- PVC cleaner
- 6 eyebolts, $3/_8 \times 6$ inches
- 6 flat washers, hex nuts and cap nuts, for eyebolts
- 15-foot chain, 750-lb test
- 6 connecting links or S hooks

- 6 yards canvas, 36 inches wide
- 6 yards fringe
- Heavy-duty thread to match canvas and fringe
- 2 pieces 18-inch cord
- Seat and back cushions

Tools required

- Handsaw
- Rubber mallet
- Chalk line
- Drill press with 1-inch bit and circle cutter
- 1-inch sanding drum
- Drill with $1/8$-and $3/8$-inch bits
- Sandpaper
- Sewing machine

Instructions

A-frame

1. Measure, cut, and label the straight pipe as listed. Sand any burrs off the ends of each pipe piece.
2. Dry-assemble the A-frame base and attach the two upright sections as shown in FIGS. 11-1 and 11-2.

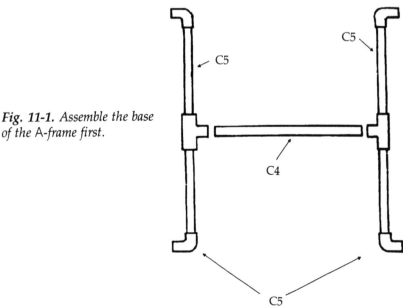

Fig. 11-1. Assemble the base of the A-frame first.

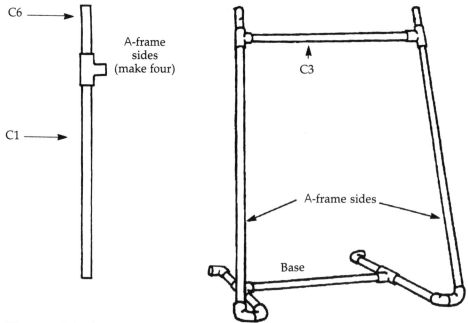

Fig. 11-2. *Join the side pieces to the base.*

Canopy frame

3. Drill two 1/2-inch holes 7 inches from each end of a C2 piece as shown in FIG. 11-3. Insert an eyebolt into each of these holes.
4. Dry-assemble the canopy top, putting the piece with the eyebolts into the center position. Refer to FIG. 11-4.

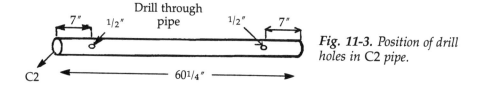

Fig. 11-3. *Position of drill holes in C2 pipe.*

Canopy

5. Cut the canvas into two 3-yard lengths. Place them together wrong side out. Fold each of the 18-inch lengths of cord in half and place the folded edge at the corners in the seam area. Stitch a seam along one 3-yard edge, catching the folded cord ends in that seam. See FIG. 11-5.
6. With the canvas wrong side out, put it on the canopy frame and pin each corner to form an angled dart. Stitch these darts. See FIG. 11-6.
7. With the cover right side out, put it back on the frame and mark a hemline. Either sew the hem or cut at that line and stick fringe along the edge.

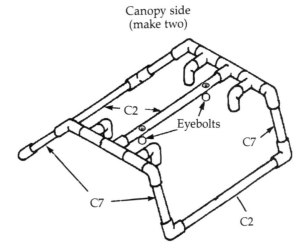

Fig. 11-4. *Assembly of the canopy frame. Note: Four C8 pieces are not shown in the top illustration, and none are shown in the bottom illustration; insert them where indicated (top).*

Canopy side (make two)

Fig. 11-5. *Canvas pattern for the canopy.*

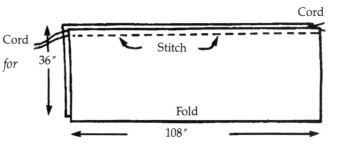

Fig. 11-6. *Fold and pin the corners, then sew the seams.*

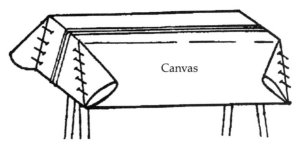

Completing frame and canopy

8. Cement the base assembly, the upright straight pipe pieces and tee assembly, and finally the upright crossbars. Also cement the canopy frame pieces. See FIG. 11-7.

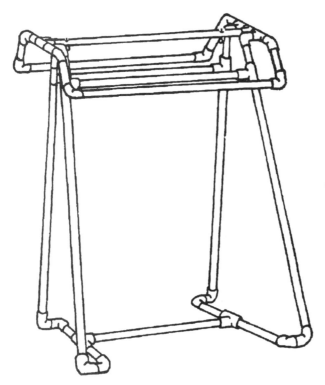

Fig. 11-7. Final assembly of the A-frame and canopy frame.

9. You will probably need assistance to finish the cementing process from here on. Dry-assemble the upright sections with the canopy frame and base assemblies. Have someone hold the canopy in position while you knock apart and cement each of the joints where the uprights connect to the base. Keeping these uprights at their proper angle to fit the canopy is crucial.

10. When the uprights are bonded to the base, cement their connections to the canopy frame, and attach the canvas cover.

Swing

11. To make the swing, take the pieces marked S1 and measure the positions for drilling the 1-inch holes to hold the 3/4-inch pipe. I suggest you start with the seat front crossbar, find the center and mark it for the first hole. Then measure 3³/4 inches to either side of the center mark until you have a series of nine holes marked, including the center hole. Measure and mark two additional locations for holes 2⁵/8 inches to the left and right of the last hole posi-

tions, for a total of 11 holes. Mark the next S1 pipe with the same hole positions by aligning it with the first pipe. Make certain the holes are in a straight line. Refer to FIG. 11-8.

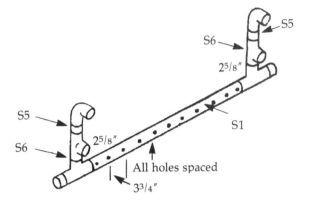

Fig. 11-8. *The front section of the swing, with the drill holes marked. Note: S6 pieces are not shown in this illustration; insert them where indicated.*

12. This second S1 piece will be the seat back lower (center) crossbar. It will have a second line of only 10 holes along the top, spaced midway between the first hole locations and about a quarter turn around the pipe as shown in FIG. 11-9. These holes will hold the back pipe spindles.

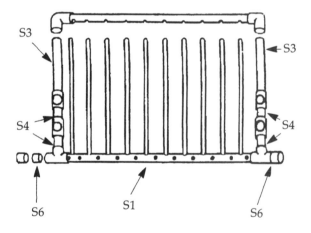

Fig. 11-9. *Back assembly of the swing.*

13. The third S1 piece will be the seat back upper crossbar. It should be marked for a line of 10 holes matching those from step 11 on the center crossbar. See FIG. 11-10.

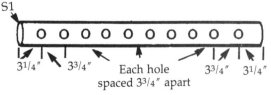

Fig. 11-10. *The top bar of the swing back, with the drill holes marked.*

14. Using a 1-inch bit, drill the holes into the pipe from above. Drill into one side of the pipe only, not through the other sidewall. Depending on the actual outside thickness of the 3/4-inch pipe, you might have to enlarge the holes slightly. Use a small 1-inch sanding drum inserted into a drill.

15. Dry-assemble the pipe pieces and fittings needed to make the swing seat, starting with the arm rests. Follow FIG. 11-11.

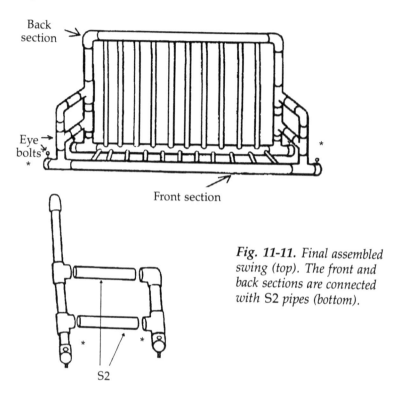

Back section

Eye bolts

Front section

Fig. 11-11. Final assembled swing (top). The front and back sections are connected with S2 pipes (bottom).

S2

16. Insert the 3/4-inch pipe pieces into the center crossbar first, then add the front and upper seat back crossbars and arm rest assemblies. The 3/4-inch pipe should fit snugly in the holes drilled for them in the three crossbars.

17. When you are certain the pieces all fit properly and everything seems correct, begin cementing the pieces together by knocking each joint apart starting at the top, and applying the cement. Gradually work your way to the bottom. All fittings must fit at perfect 90-degree angles, otherwise your project will be lopsided.

18. To prepare the swing for hanging, drill a 3/8-inch hole straight down and all the way through each end cap already cemented in position. Insert the eyebolts and secure with the washers, hex nuts, and cap nuts.

19. Make the chain connectors as shown in FIG. 11-12 and attach to the eyebolts.

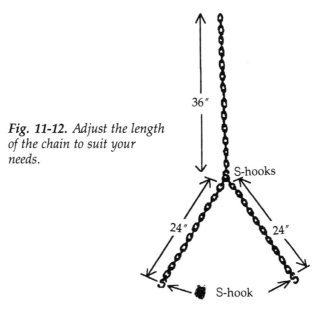

Fig. 11-12. *Adjust the length of the chain to suit your needs.*

20. Using the cleaner, remove all marks from the pipe. If you plan to paint it, the pipe must be sanded thoroughly to roughen the shiny surface.
21. Standard yard furniture replacement cushions will fit this project for both the seat and back.
22. Enjoy a relaxing swing with a friend.

12

Computer desk and chair

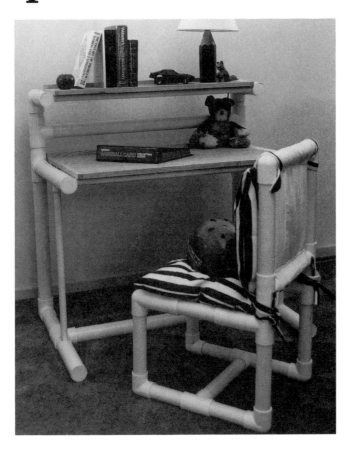

The design of this project is amazingly simple, yet good-looking and functional. You can enlarge this desk to hold both a printer and computer, or keep it this size, which is perfect for a word processor. This project will look good in the den or in the children's room for a study desk. You can paint this project bright decorator colors or leave it the color of the white pipe. In any event, it is bound to get plenty of use.

Materials

Desk

- 2-inch PVC pipe, 15 feet long (1-inch fitting allowance), cut to size as follows:

  2 pieces 24 inches long (D1)

  2 pieces $22^1/2$ inches long (D2)

  4 pieces 3 inches long (D3)

  2 pieces 12 inches long (D4)

  2 pieces $9^1/2$ inches long (D5)

  2 pieces 8 inches long (D6)

  2 pieces 35 inches long (D9)

- $3/4$-inch PVC pipe, 18 feet long, cut to size as follows:

  2 pieces $28^1/4$ inches long (D7)

  4 pieces 39 inches long (D8)

- 2-inch fittings:

  4 elbows, 90 degrees

  6 tees

- $3^3/4$-inch oak wood core plywood:

  1 piece $22^1/2 \times 33^1/2$ inches, desktop

  1 piece $8^1/2 \times 33^1/2$ inches, shelf

- $3/4$-inch oak wood strips:

  2 pieces $1^1/2 \times 35$ inches, lip

  2 pieces $3/4 \times 35$ inches, front lip

  2 pieces $8^1/2$ inches, shelf sides

  2 pieces $22^1/2$ inches, desk sides

Chair

- $1^1/2$-inch PVC pipe, 14 feet long ($3/4$-inch fitting allowance), cut to size as follows:

  2 pieces $7^1/2$ inches long (C1)

  4 pieces $16^1/2$ inches long (C2)

  4 pieces $6^1/2$ inches long (C3)

  2 pieces 14 inches long (C4)

  5 pieces 13 inches long (C5)

- $1^1/2$-inch fittings:

  8 elbows, 90 degrees

  8 tees

Hardware and miscellaneous

- PVC cement
- Silicone glue

- 1 yard 36-inch wide white fabric or canvas, for the sling
- 1 yard colored canvas, for the cushion
- Matching heavy-duty thread
- Carpenter's wood glue
- 30 wood screws, 1½-inch
- 24 wood plugs, ½-inch, oak
- 6 wood circles, ¾×2 inches
- 1 pint paint, white gloss enamel
- Seat cushions

Tools required

- Handsaw
- Rubber mallet
- Drill with ⅛- and 1-inch bits and ½-inch countersink bit and 1-inch drum sander
- Circular saw
- Circle cutter, 2-inch capability
- Screwdriver
- Pad or belt sander
- Sewing machine

Instructions

Chair

1. Measure, cut, and label the straight pipe pieces as listed.
2. Dry-assemble the chair first on a flat surface. Assemble each side section, forming mirror images. Attach the center pieces and make certain the chair does not rock and is flat against the floor. See FIG. 12-1.

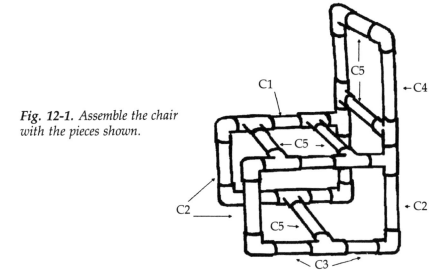

Fig. 12-1. Assemble the chair with the pieces shown.

3. Disassemble and reassemble the side sections of the chair using cement. Do not attach the center pieces at this time. Set aside.

Desk

4. To begin the desk assembly, measure and mark drill points 3 inches from the ends of the 2-inch pipes marked D1. These holes will hold the $3/4$-inch pipes labeled D8 that support the desktop. Make certain these points are in a straight line. Mark a drill point 10 inches from the end of the pipe marked D4 and 10 inches from the end, on the bottom front, of the one marked D1. Refer to FIG. 12-2. The assembly must be tight with no slack or wobble.

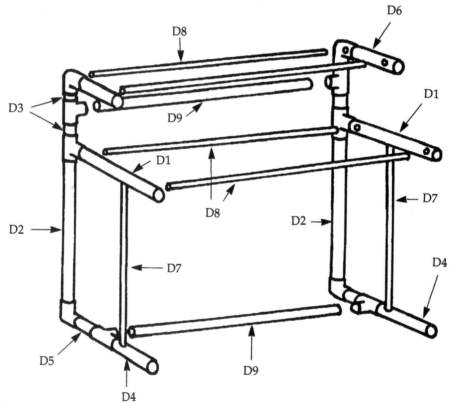

Fig. 12-2. Assemble the desk as shown.

5. Cement the two pipe pieces marked D6 into two 2-inch elbows. Measure and mark a drill point 2 inches from the front of the D6 pipe and in the center of the 2-inch elbows as shown in FIG. 12-2.
6. Drill 1-inch holes into the D1, D4, D6, and elbow pipes marked in steps 4 and 5. Enlarge the holes slightly if needed using a 1-inch drum sander inserted into a handheld power drill.

7. Dry-assemble the desk on a flat surface as shown in FIG. 12-2. Double-check to make certain that all pieces fit together properly and the desk sits flat on the floor. The pipe piece marked D7 should be long enough to support the D1 piece. Make certain to allow no slack, or the front of the desk might tilt forward.

If you plan to use the desk for writing, the overall height should be 27 to 29 inches tall to the desk writing surface. If you plan to use it to hold a computer or for typing, a height of 24 to 25 inches is better. See FIG. 12-3.

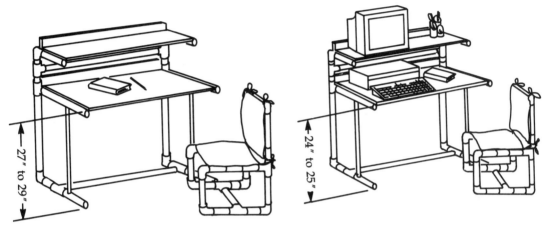

Fig. 12-3. *For a writing desk (left), use a height of 27 to 29 inches. For a computer desk (right), try a height of 24 to 25 inches.*

8. Knock down the side pieces and reassemble them using cement. Complete the assembly by adding the D8 and D9 center pieces.

Desktop and shelf

9. Measure and cut the desk shelf and top from $3/4$-inch oak wood core plywood using a circular saw with a plywood fine-tooth blade. The shelf is $8^1/2 \times 33^1/2$ inches and the top is $22^1/2 \times 33^1/2$ inches. See FIG. 12-4.
10. Measure and cut the $3/4$-inch oak strips to size.
11. Drill holes into the wood strips (FIG. 12-5), and attach the strips to the shelf and top sides with glue and countersunk screws.
12. Glue $1/2$-inch wood plugs into the countersunk screw holes, and sand flush to the wood strip surface.
13. Using a circle cutter, cut six 2-inch wood circles from $3/4$-inch scrap wood stock. Paint the pieces white to match the color of the pipe. Allow to dry thoroughly.
14. Glue the wood circles into the exposed 2-inch pipe ends with silicone.
15. Drill $1/8$-inch holes 3 inches from each end of the D8 pipe center pieces. Position the shelf and the top the way you want them and fasten to the pipe by

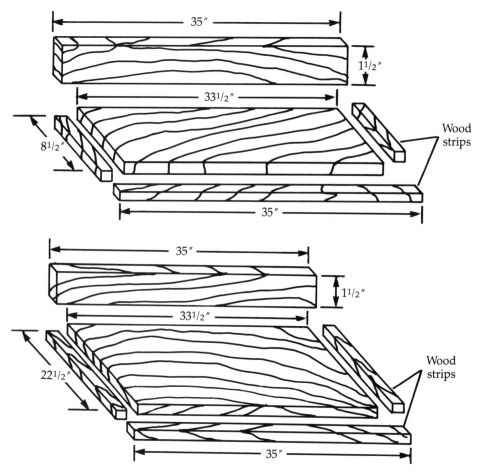

Fig. 12-4. Construction of the desktop and shelf.

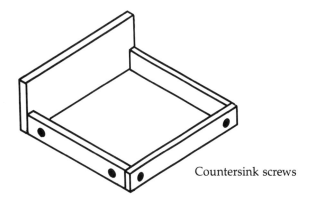

Fig. 12-5. Attach the wood strips to the desktop and shelf with glue and countersunk screws.

Countersink screws

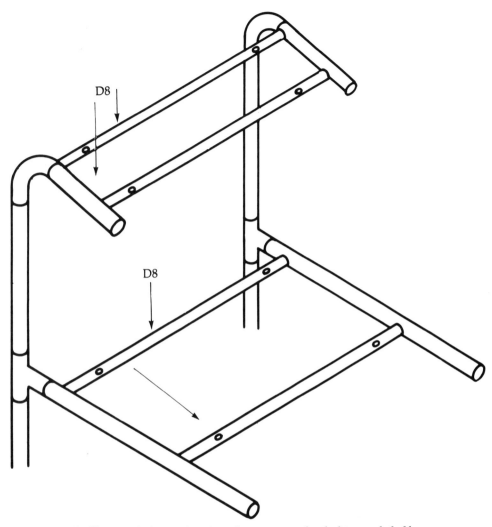

Fig. 12-6. Drill screw holes in the pipes that support the desktop and shelf.

placing screws through the pipe into the bottom of the shelf and top. See FIG. 12-6.

Slings

16. Measure and cut the sling material for the back and seat of the chair as shown in FIG. 12-7. The sides of the slings should be hemmed 1/2- to 1-inch deep. Allow 6 inches at each end to wrap around the 1 1/2-inch pipe.

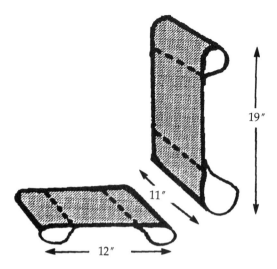

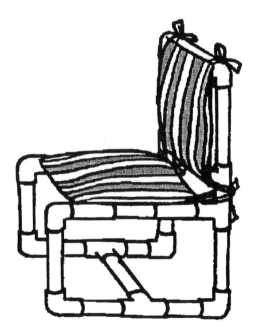

Fig. 12-7. Measure and cut sling material.

17. Slip the sling over the center pipe of the chair, and cement the pipe into position. Add cushions that you've bought or made. See FIG. 12-8.

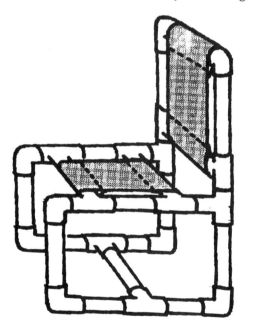

Fig. 12-8. Make a canvas sling for the chair.

13

Chaise chair
with footstool and table

This lounging combination is one of the most comfortable you will ever experience. The tilt of the chaise chair and footstool combine in a unique way to bring a whole new meaning to relaxing on the patio or deck. The table is just the right height to hold your favorite drink and snack, too. Imagine lounging in this combination while your neighbors watch with envy.

Materials

Chaise

- $1^1/_2$-inch PVC pipe, 30 feet long ($^7/_8$-inch fitting allowance), cut to size as follows:
  4 pieces 24 inches long (C1)
  2 pieces $20^3/_4$ inches long (C2)
  2 pieces 14 inches long (C3)
  2 pieces 7 inches long (C4)
  2 pieces $12^1/_2$ inches long (C5)
  2 pieces $5^1/_2$ inches long (C6)
  2 pieces $14^1/_2$ inches long (C7)
  4 pieces 14 inches long (C8)
  4 pieces $2^1/_4$ inches long (C9)
  10 pieces $1^3/_4$ inches long (C10)
- $1^1/_2$-inch fittings:
  10 elbows, 90 degrees
  16 tees

Footstool

- $1^1/_2$-inch PVC pipe, 10 feet ($^7/_8$-inch fitting allowance)
  2 pieces, 10 inches long (S1)
  2 pieces, 12 inches long (S2)
  6 pieces, $1^3/_4$ inches long (S3)
  4 pieces, 14 inches long (S4)
- $1^1/_2$-inch fittings:
  6 elbows, 90 degrees
  2 elbows, 45 degrees
  4 tees

Table

- $1^1/_2$-inch PVC pipe, 14 feet long ($^7/_8$-inch fitting allowance), cut to size as follows:
  2 pieces 10 inches long (T1)
  4 pieces $9^3/_4$ inches long (T2)
  2 pieces 13 inches long (T3)
  4 pieces $8^1/_2$ inches long (T4)
  4 pieces 11 inches long (T5)
- $1^1/_2$-inch fittings:
  4 elbows, 90 degrees
  8 tees
  4 end caps

- $1/4$-inch acrylic sheet, white, sized as follows:
  1 piece 10×10 inches
  1 piece $9^3/4 \times 18^1/4$ inches
- $3/4$-inches wood stock:
  8 pieces $3/4 \times 2$ inches

Hardware and miscellaneous

- Canvas 15×90 inches
- Matching heavy-duty thread
- PVC cement
- 8 screws, Dacrotized, $1^1/2$ inches
- PVC cleaner
- Cushions

Tools required

- Rubber mallet
- Drill with $1/8$-inch bit
- Drill press with circle cutter
- Handsaw
- Circular saw with a fine-tooth blade
- Sewing machine

Instructions

Footstool and chair

1. Measure, cut, and label the straight pipe pieces as listed.
2. Dry-assemble the pieces for the footstool on a flat surface as shown in FIG. 13-1.

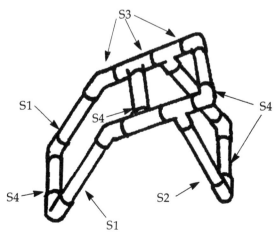

Fig. 13-1. Assemble the footstool as shown. Note: S3 pieces are not shown in this illustration; insert them where indicated.

3. Dry-assemble the pieces for the chaise by first making the sides mirror images, and then the chair insides. See FIG. 13-2.

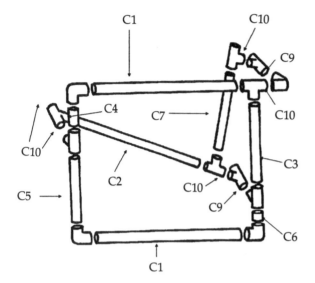

Fig. 13-2. Assemble the chaise with the pieces shown. Note: C9 and C10 pieces are not shown in this illustration; insert them where indicated.

4. Knock down the assemblies and remove the marks from the pipe and fittings.
5. Measure and cut the canvas pieces that form the slings for both the stool and the chair as follows:

    The sling for the stool is 13 inches wide after hemming and $12^1/2$ inches long, with an 8-inch loop at each end to go over the center pipe, for a total finished length of $20^1/2$ inches.

    The bottom sling for the chair is 14 inches wide after hemming and 32 inches long, inclusive of 8-inch loops at both ends for a total finished length of 40 inches.

    The back sling is 14 inches wide after hemming and 23 inches long, with an 8-inch loop at one end for a total finished length of 27 inches.

    Sew the back sling into the bottom sling 9 inches from its end to be in line with the angle of the back. See FIG. 13-3.
6. Reassemble the footstool and the chaise sides so they are mirror images. Cement and adjust the fittings to a 90-degree angle quickly before the joint sets, fusing the two pieces.
7. Attach the center pieces to the footstool with the sling in the top two center pipe pieces as shown in FIG. 13-4. If you want to disassemble the unit later, I suggest you use sheet-metal screws to hold the center pipe in place. Otherwise, use cement. Make certain the final assembly is done on a level surface.
8. Assemble the center portion of the chair, inserting the sling between the front and back lower and upper center pipe pieces as shown in FIG. 13-5. If you wish to disassemble the chair for storage later, use sheet-metal screws to

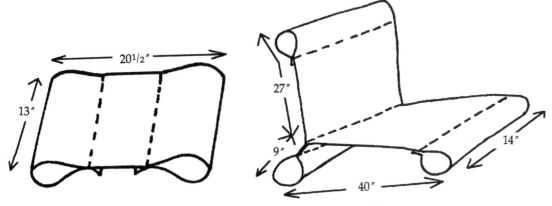

Fig. 13-3. *Canvas sling patterns for the footstool (left) and chaise (right).*

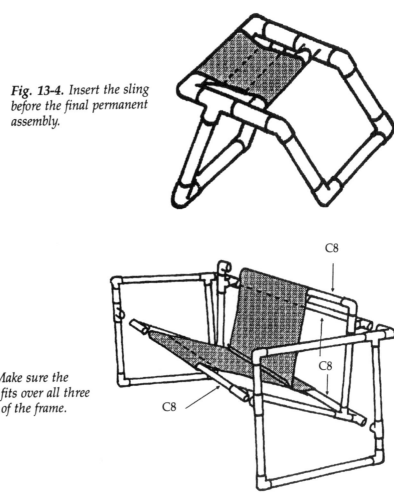

Fig. 13-4. *Insert the sling before the final permanent assembly.*

Fig. 13-5. *Make sure the chaise sling fits over all three center pipes of the frame.*

hold the center pipe in place. If not, use cement. Make certain the assembly is done on a flat surface and the chair does not rock.

Table

9. One side of each of four tees for the table requires a hole to fit the 1¹/₂-inch pipe. This hole should be about 1⁷/₈ inches. You will need a drill press and circle cutter to create the hole. Position the tee so it is centered under the circle cutter properly. Clamp the fitting in place before attempting to drill the hole. The hole should be aligned at a 90-degree angle to the other side fitting opening. Drill the hole at a slow to moderate speed. See FIG. 13-6.

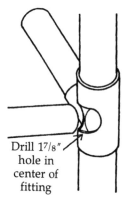

Drill 1⁷/₈″ hole in center of fitting

Fig. 13-6. Drill a hole in the double tee to hold the connecting pipe pieces.

10. Dry-assemble the table pieces on a flat surface following FIG. 13-7.

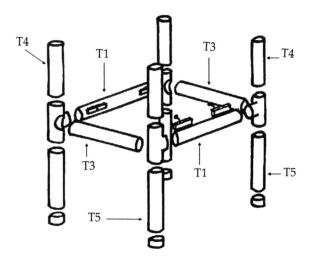

T4 T1 T3 T4

T3 T1 T5

T5

Fig. 13-7. Assemble the table frame with the pieces shown.

11. Knock down the assembly and clean the pipe and fittings.
12. Measure and cut the white acrylic sheet to size. Sand the edges to remove all rough edges.

13. Measure and cut the wood strips two inches long.
14. Using 1¹/₂-inch screws, attach the wood strips to the inside lower portion of the two levels of the table as shown in FIG. 13-8.

Fig. 13-8. Attach wood strips to the table assembly to serve as supports for the tabletops.

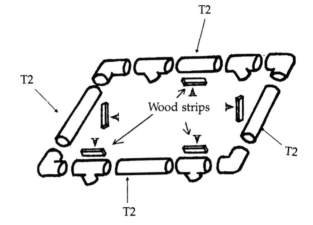

15. Reassemble the table on a flat surface using cement.
16. Lay the acrylic pieces onto the wood supports.
17. Purchase cushions to fit the chaise and footstool, or make your own.

14

Modern table and chairs

This project is designed for use inside your home but will also look great on the patio or deck. You can leave the pipe white or paint it black for a sleek look. No matter which color you choose, this project is one that is practical and relatively easy to make in a weekend.

Materials

Chairs

Multiply the figures below by the number of chairs you wish to make.

- $1^1/_2$-inch PVC pipe, 20 feet long ($^7/_8$-inch fitting allowance), cut to size as follows:
  2 pieces 21 inches long (C1)
  2 pieces 16 inches long (C2)
  2 pieces $14^1/_2$ inches long (C3)
  2 pieces 12 inches long (C4)
  2 pieces $14^1/_2$ inches long (C5)
  2 pieces $10^1/_2$ inches long (C6)
  2 pieces 8 inches long (C7)
  2 pieces $3^3/_4$ inches long (C8)
  13 pieces $1^3/_4$ inches long (C9)
  1 piece 7 inches long (C10)
- $1^1/_2$-inch fittings, cut to size as follows:
  6 elbows, 90 degrees
  4 elbows, 45 degrees
  12 tees
  4 end caps

Table

- 2 inch PVC pipe, 20 feet long ($1^1/_4$-inch fitting allowance), cut to size as follows:
  4 pieces 20 inches long (T1)
  2 pieces 16 inches long (T2)
  2 pieces $8^1/_4$ inches long (T3)
  4 pieces $19^3/_4$ inches long (T4)
  12 pieces $2^1/_2$ inches long (T5)
- 2-inch fittings:
  4 elbows, 90 degrees
  12 tees
  4 end caps

Hardware and miscellaneous

- 2 yards canvas for fabric slings
- Matching heavy-duty thread
- 1 piece $^1/_2$-inch glass, to fit completed table top space
- PVC cement
- PVC cleaner

Tools required

- Rubber mallet
- Handsaw
- Sewing machine

Instructions

Chairs and slings

1. Measure, cut, and label the $1^1/_2$-inch pipe pieces for the chair.
2. Dry-assemble the parts for each chair on a level and flat surface as shown in FIG. 14-1.

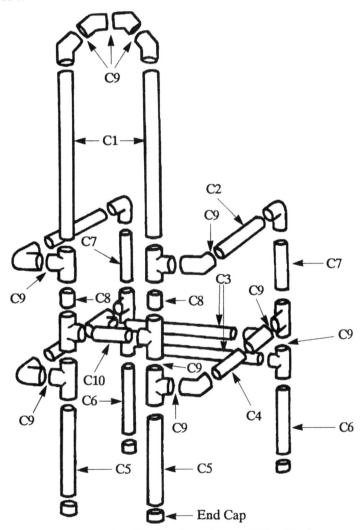

Fig. 14-1. *Assemble the chair with the pieces shown. Note: C9 pieces are not shown in this illustration; insert them where indicated.*

3. Measure and cut the canvas sling material for the seat and back of each chair according to the following dimensions, but be certain to fit each to the chair to leave no sagging. The size for the back sling is 9 inches wide with a 1/2-inch hem, and 18 1/2 inches long with a 7-inch loop at each end to fit over the pipe, for a finished length of 11 1/2 inches. The seat sling is 10 inches wide with a 1/2-inch hem, and 26 1/2 inches long with a 7-inch loop at each end, for a finished length of 19 1/2 inches. See FIG. 14-2.

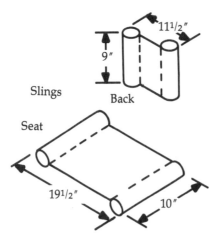

Fig. 14-2. Sling patterns for the back and seat of the chair.

4. Clean the pipe and fittings to remove all markings.
5. Reassemble the pipe and fittings and slings as shown in FIG. 14-3, cementing all connections. Remember to do the assembly on a flat surface.

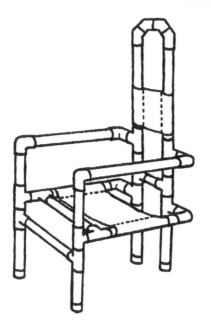

Fig. 14-3. Be sure to slide the slings into place before you cement the final assembly.

Table

6. Measure, cut, and label the straight 2-inch pipe for the table.
7. Dry-assemble the table as shown in FIG. 14-4 on a flat surface.

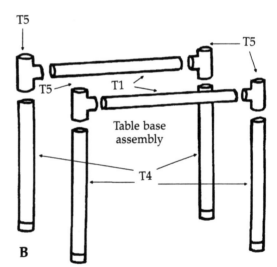

Fig. 14-4. Assemble the tabletop (top) and base (bottom) with the pieces shown. Note: T5 pieces are not shown in this illustration; insert them where indicated.

8. Remove the markings from the pipe and fittings.
9. Reassemble the table using pipe cement.
10. The tabletop can be glass, wood, or laminated particle board. I felt glass would look the best for this furniture design. You can buy glass tops in ovals or squares or circles. Pick the form you like best and purchase according to the measured dimensions of your tabletop space.
11. You can purchase replacement cushions at most discount centers or make your own. You will need the kind with ties for the backrest of the chairs.

15

Loft bed/desk/closet

This unique design is both functional and efficient. It allows you to use the space under the loft bed to store clothing, and incorporates a desk your child can use well into his or her early teens. It's modern look is sure to get lots of compliments from visiting friends.

Materials

Loft bed/desk

- 2-inch PVC pipe, 80 feet (1$1/4$-inch fitting allowance), cut to size as follows:
  7 pieces 37 inches long (P1)
  2 pieces 53 inches long (P2)
  4 pieces 4$1/4$ inches long (P3)
  6 pieces 4 inches long (P4)
  4 pieces 2$1/2$ inches long (P5)
  1 piece 70 inches long (P6)
  1 piece 52 inches long (P7)
  1 piece 10 inches long (P8)
  2 pieces 13 $3/4$ inches long (P9)
  2 pieces 13 inches long (P10)
  2 pieces 22$1/2$ inches long (P11)
  4 pieces 26 inches long (P12)
  2 pieces 24 inches long (P13)
  8 pieces 14$1/2$ inches long (P14)

- 1$1/2$-inch PVC pipe, 17 feet ($3/4$-inch fitting allowance), cut to size as follows:
  2 pieces 4 inches long (P15)
  4 pieces 2 inches long (P16)
  10 pieces 6 inches long (P17)
  6 pieces 10 inches long (P18)
  2 pieces 12$1/2$ inches long (P19)
  1 piece 37 inches long (P20)

- $3/4$-inch PVC pipe, 7 feet:
  2 pieces 40 inches long (P21)

- 2-inch fittings:
  12 elbows, 90 degrees
  26 tees
  4 adapters, 1$1/2$ to 2 inches

- 1$1/2$-inch fittings:
  2 elbows, 90 degrees
  4 elbows, 45 degrees
  12 tees
  2 end caps

- $3/4$-inch red oak plywood:
  1 piece 24 × 35$1/2$ inches

- $3/4$-inch red oak lumber:
  2 pieces $3/4$ × $3/4$ × 24 inches
  2 pieces $3/4$ × 1$1/2$ × 20 inches
  1 piece $3/4$ × $3/4$ × 37 inches
  1 piece $3/4$ × 2 × 38 inches

Chair

- 1¹/2-inch PVC pipe, 11 feet, cut to size as follows:
  2 pieces 13 inches long (P22)
  4 pieces 12¹/4 inches long (P23)
  2 pieces 7³/4 inches long (P24)
  4 pieces 6³/4 inches long (P25)
- ¹/2-inch fittings:
  8 elbows, 90 degrees
  6 tees

Hardware and miscellaneous

- 2 pints PVC cement
- 1 gallon PVC cleaner
- ¹/2 yard canvas for sling
- Matching heavy-duty thread
- 3 yards canvas mattress support
- 8 screws, 1¹/2 inches
- 8 red oak wood plugs, ¹/2 inch
- Carpenter's glue
- 4 molly bolts, 2 inches
- 1 pint Danish oil stain

Tools required

- Handsaw
- Circular saw
- Drill with ¹/2-inch countersink and ¹/2-inch bit and flap-wheel sander
- Screwdriver
- Sewing machine

Instructions

Chair and sling

1. Measure, cut, and label the straight pipe across as listed.
2. Dry-assemble the chair on a flat surface, as shown in FIG. 15-1. Assemble each side section, forming mirror images. Attach the center pieces labeled P22 and make certain the chair does not rock and is flat to the floor. Knock down the assembly.
3. Reassemble only the side pieces using PVC cement. Insert the P22 center pieces but do not cement. Remove all markings from the pipe. Set aside.
4. Measure and cut the sling material from the canvas according to the measurements given in FIG. 15-2. Hem the edges ¹/2 inch, and the rolls at each end to slide over two of the center pieces of pipe P22.

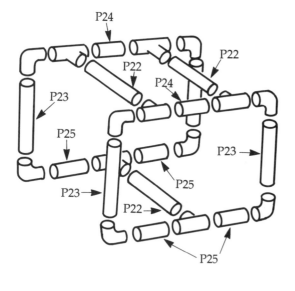

Fig. 15-1. *Assemble the chair with the pieces shown.*

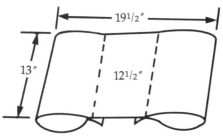

Fig. 15-2. *Canvas sling pattern for the chair seat.*

5. Slide the sling over the two center pieces P22 as shown in FIG. 15-3, and cement the pipe in place.

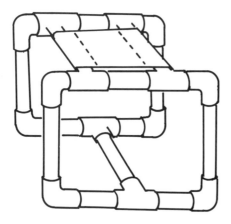

Fig. 15-3. *Place the sling over the center pipes.*

Loft bed/desk

6. Dry-assemble the side pieces of the bunk bed/desk combination on a large flat table or a floor you know is flat. You must use two 2-inch to 1¹/₂-inch adapter fittings for the 90-degree elbows that hold the clothes rod (P20), and two for the tee fittings to which the ladder is attached (P15). See FIG. 15-4. Attach the center pieces (P1) and make any necessary final adjustments. Knock apart the assembly.

7. Reassemble the sides this time using PVC cement. You might need some help for this step.

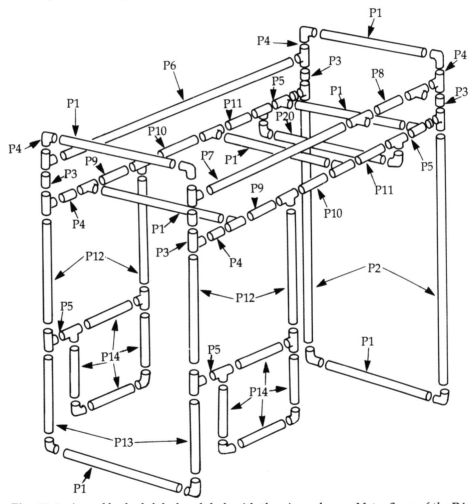

Fig. 15-4. *Assemble the loft bed and desk with the pieces shown. Note: Some of the P4 pieces and all of the P5 pieces are not shown in this illustration; insert them where indicated.*

Sling

8. Measure and cut the canvas mattress support material according to the following measurements. You want to create a piece that is 34 inches wide, with a 1/2-inch hem included. Cut the material 88 inches long and form 9-inch loops at both ends to fit over the center pipe pieces (P1) that support the mattress. I suggest you make one loop first and then custom-fit the last loop so the canvas fits tightly with no sagging. If you child is heavier than 200 pounds, you might want to consider using 1/2-inch plywood instead of the sling.

9. Reassemble the bed using PVC cement to hold the center pieces in place (FIG. 15-5). Do this final assembly in your child's room. If you ever move the assembly to another room, you will have to cut the center pieces and reassemble with sleeve fittings. You must have all joints tightly cemented to form a solid piece of furniture.

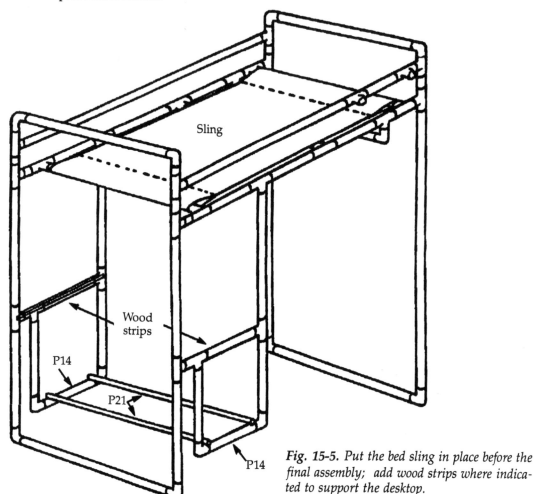

Sling

Wood strips

P14

P21

P14

Fig. 15-5. Put the bed sling in place before the final assembly; add wood strips where indicated to support the desktop.

10. Attach the two pieces of 3/4-inch pipe labeled P21 to the pipes at the bottom of the desk area labeled P14: Drill a 1/2-inch hole 1/2 inch from each end into one side of the P21 pipe. Drill a screw starter hole in the other side, at both ends. Attach with 3/4-inch screws and cement (FIG. 15-5). This piece is designed to hold a plastic laundry basket, or you can make a wood box to slide on the pipes as a storage drawer.

Desktop

11. Measure and cut the 3/4-inch red oak plywood to size. Measure and cut the red oak lumber trim pieces. See FIG. 15-6.

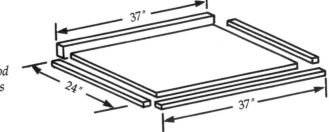

Fig. 15-6. *Cut the plywood and trim pieces to the sizes indicated.*

12. Attach the trim pieces to the plywood as shown in FIG. 15-7 using glue and 1 1/2-inch screws. Countersink the drill holes and fill with wood plugs.

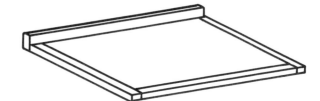

Fig. 15-7. *Attach the trim pieces to the plywood.*

13. Stain the desktop the color of your choice. I used a walnut-colored Danish oil.
14. Attach the 3/4- x 1 1/2-inch wood strips to the side of the pipe that forms the edge of the desktop. Use molly bolts to hold the strips in place. Attach the desktop and hold in place with screws from underneath the wood strips (see FIG. 15-5).
15. This last step is an absolute must: Firmly attach one side of the structure, not an end, to a wall in your child's room. Secure the bed in place with metal or nylon straps molly bolted into the wall or, preferably, studs. Do not attempt to use this project as a stand-alone piece. It is top heavy and will fall over.

Ladder

16. Dry-assemble the ladder on a flat surface using the 1 1/2-inch pipe and fittings as indicated in FIG. 15-8. Attach the ladder to the bed and make any necessary

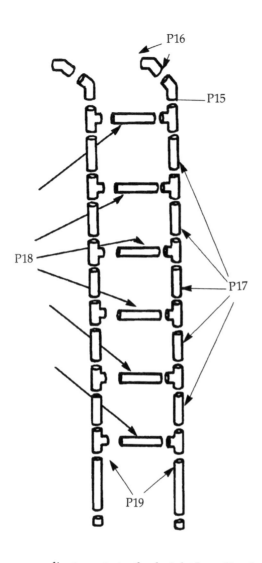

Fig. 15-8. Assemble the ladder with the pieces shown. Note: P16 pieces are not shown in this illustration; insert them where indicated.

adjustments to the height by adjusting the length of the bottom pipe (P19). Dry assemble.

17. Reassemble the ladder using cement. Attach to the bed using cement.

16

Planter bench

What could be nicer than having a planter bench on your patio or back porch? This project requires wood, PVC pipe, and fittings to create an unusual item that is both functional and decorative. Allow a weekend for this project, and you will be pleasantly surprised by how fast it goes together.

Materials

- 1^1/$_2$-inch PVC pipe, 30 feet (^{7}/$_8$-inch fitting allowance), cut to size as follows:
  2 pieces 37^1/$_2$ inches long (P1)
  8 pieces 16 inches long (P2)
  8 pieces 12 inches long (P3)
  4 pieces 7 inches long (P4)
  8 pieces 1^3/$_4$ inches long (P5)

- 1^1/$_2$-inch fittings:
  12 elbows, 90 degrees
  12 tees

- ^{1}/$_2$-inch pressure-treated plywood:
  4 pieces 13^1/$_2$ × 14 inches
  4 pieces 14 × 14^1/$_2$ inches
  4 pieces 13^1/$_2$ × 13^1/$_2$ inches

- 2-×-4 pressure treated lumber:
  16 pieces 1^1/$_2$ × 15^1/$_2$ inches
  8 pieces 1^1/$_2$ × 12 inches

Hardware and miscellaneous

- 1 yard canvas material for sling
- Matching heavy-duty thread
- Seat cushions
- 80 galvanized finishing nails, 1 inch long
- PVC cement
- PVC cleaner
- Clear silicone glue
- 1 pint exterior white paint

Tools required

- Rubber mallet
- Hammer
- Table or radial saw
- Paintbrush
- Sewing machine

Instructions

Bench frame

1. Measure, cut, and label the straight pipe as listed.
2. Assemble all pieces and dry-assemble the planter bench frame as shown in FIG. 16-1. Make the right side first. Then make a left side mirror image. Join the two with the 37^1/$_2$-inch pipes labeled P1. See FIG. 16-2.

This computer console project is a must for that office at home.

A compact glider swing is perfect for a garden apartment or a deck.

A six-station feeder will keep your backyard filled with grateful birds, especially in the cold months.

This attractive umbrella stand will hold several umbrellas, as well as canes and other items often needed at the front door.

You'll probably want to make more than one bookcase, as they are functional in every room in the house.

A fun and inexpensive project for newlyweds, this modern table-and-chairs set is easy to make.

You don't have to paint any-thing this elaborate to get some appreciation from the local wren population. Make several and draw a crowd.

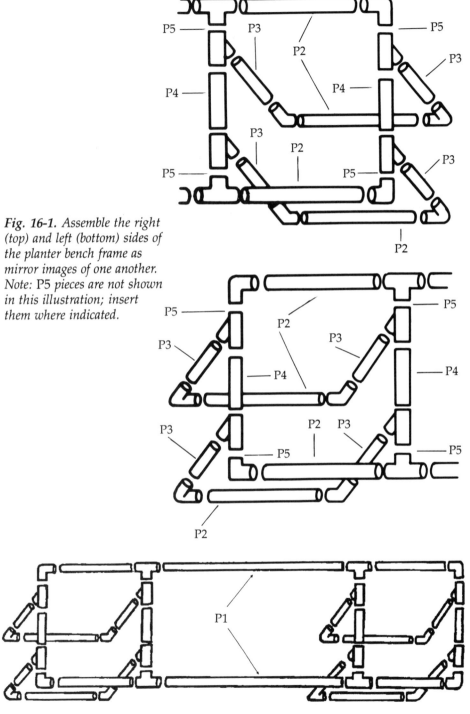

Fig. 16-1. Assemble the right (top) and left (bottom) sides of the planter bench frame as mirror images of one another. Note: P5 pieces are not shown in this illustration; insert them where indicated.

Fig. 16-2. Connect the two sides with P1 pipes.

3. Using cleaner, remove the markings from the pipe and fittings.
4. Reassemble the planter bench, except for the P1 center pieces, using cement. Make certain you do this on a level, flat surface.

Planter containers

5. Measure and cut the 1/2-inch plywood to size using a table saw or radial arm saw as shown in FIG. 16-3.

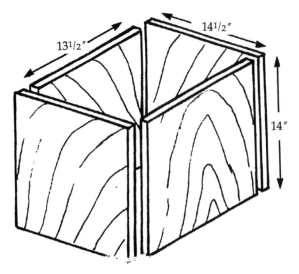

13¹/₂"   14¹/₂"

14"

Fig. 16-3. Cut the plywood for the planter boxes to the indicated sizes.

6. Measure and cut the 2×4 to size to make the trim for the planter container, an L-shaped molding that is ¹/₄-inch thick and 1¹/₂×1¹/₂ inches. Cut the top and bottom pieces with a 45 degree miter, 15¹/₂ inches long. Cut the side trim to 12-inch length. See FIG. 16-4.

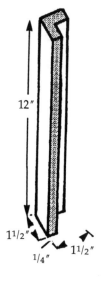

12"

1¹/₂"   1/₄"   1¹/₂"

Fig. 16-4. Make the trim for the planter boxes with 2-×-4 wood.

7. Assemble the planter containers using silicone glue and 1-inch galvanized finishing nails. Attach the trim on the top, bottom, and sides using nails and glue. See FIG. 16-5.

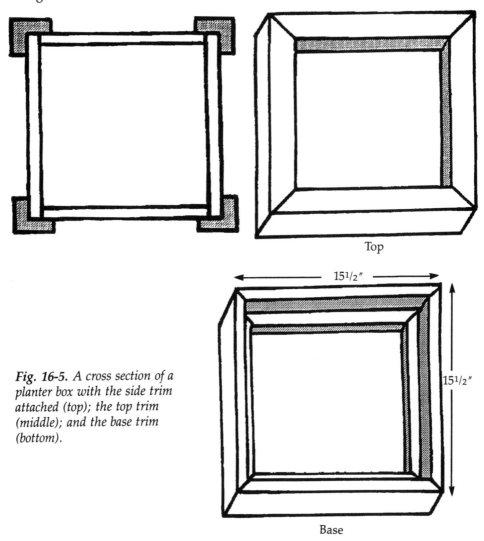

Top

Fig. 16-5. *A cross section of a planter box with the side trim attached (top); the top trim (middle); and the base trim (bottom).*

15¹/₂″

15¹/₂″

Base

8. Paint the planter boxes white to match the bench color.
9. Measure and cut the canvas to make the sling for the center of the planter bench: It is 35 inches long with a ¹/₂-inch hem on each side, and 27 inches wide, sewn with two 7-inch loops at each end, for a finished width of 20 inches. See FIG. 16-6.
10. Slip the sling over the P1 center pipes and fasten the pipes to the ends with PVC cement.

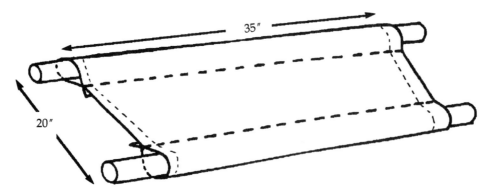

Fig. 16-6. Pattern for the bench seat's canvas sling.

11. Lower the planter boxes into each end of the planter bench and fill them with your favorite plants, bushes, or flowers.
12. The center is designed to hold a standard replacement cushion for a yard chair, which can be purchased at most home centers and discount stores.

17
Glider swing

This project is one of the most comfortable chairs you will ever experience. It is a very relaxing and soothing place just to sit, rock, listen to your favorite music, or commune with nature. The side tables add to the utility of the project for holding drinks, reading materials, and snacks. You might as well make two because you are bound to get requests for more.

Materials

Frame

- 2-inch PVC pipe, 21 feet long (1¹/₂-inch fitting allowance), cut to size as follows:
  4 pieces 12 inches long (F1)
  4 pieces 42 inches long (F2)
  2 pieces 5 inches long (F3)
  8 pieces 3 inches long (F4)
- 2-inch fittings:
  4 elbows, 90 degrees
  12 tees
  4 end caps
- 1-×-8 lumber, ³/₄ inch thick
  2 pieces 7¹/₂×24 inches, for end tables
  4 pieces 4×4 inches, for mounting blocks

Chair

- 1¹/₂-inch PVC pipe, 30 feet long (⁷/₈-inch fitting allowance), cut to size as follows:
  1 piece 19 inches long (C1)
  2 pieces 7¹/₂ inches long (C2)
  2 pieces 7 inches long (C3)
  2 pieces 26 inches long (C4)
  2 pieces 10¹/₄ inches long (C5)
  1 piece 16¹/₄ inches long (C6)
  2 pieces 20 inches long (C7)
  2 pieces 22 inches long (C8)
  1 piece 28 inches long (C9)
  2 pieces 16 inches long (C10)
  14 pieces 1³/₄ inches long (C11)
  4 pieces 2¹/₂ inches long (C12)
  2 pieces 11¹/₂ inches long (C13)
- 1¹/₂-inch fittings:
  12 elbows, 90 degrees
  10 tees
  4 double tees
  4 end caps

Hardware and miscellaneous

- PVC cleaner
- PVC cement

- Carpenter's wood glue
- 8 eyebolts, $3/8 \times 5$ inches
- 4 pieces 6-inch chain, 500-lb test
- 1 piece canvas, 20×54 inches
- Matching heavy-duty thread
- Seat cushions

Tools required

- Rubber mallet
- Handsaw
- Drill with $3/8$-inch countersink bit
- Saber saw
- Router with rounding-over bit
- Pad sander
- Sewing machine

Instructions

Frame

1. Measure and cut all straight $1 1/2$- and 2-inch pipe as listed, and label.
2. Start with the frame assembly. Dry-assemble each side so the fittings face each other. Add the center pipe. Make certain you do this assembly on a flat surface. See FIG. 17-1.

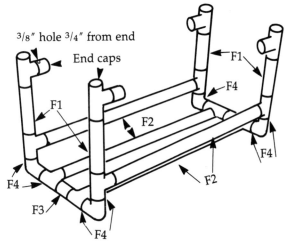

Fig. 17-1. Assemble the chair frame with the pieces shown. Note the location of the $3/8$-inch holes on the end caps. Note: F4 pieces are not shown in this illustration; insert them where indicated.

3/8" hole 3/4" from end

End caps

3. Knock apart with the mallet and reassemble the frame piece by piece, using PVC cement.
4. Drill $3/8$-inch holes into the center of the end caps, $3/4$ of an inch from the end. Attach the eyebolts with nuts and lock washers. See FIG. 17-2.

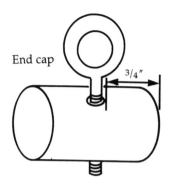

End cap

3/4"

Fig. 17-2. Drill holes in the end caps and attach the eyebolts.

5. Before trimming the mounting blocks to size, cut their centers out, making a hole large enough to fit over the open tee fittings. Then measure and cut the wood tabletops that fit on the end of the frame. See FIG. 17-3.

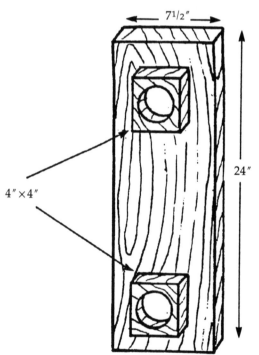

7 1/2"

24"

4" × 4"

Fig. 17-3. Cut the center out of the 4- × -4-inch mounting blocks to fit over open tee fittings; then attach the blocks to the tabletops.

6. Slip two wood mounting blocks onto the open fitting ends on each side of the frame. Center a tabletop over the wood blocks and glue and clamp together. This method is the best way to ensure that the blocks are centered properly over the tee fittings and under the tabletop. When the glue has set, remove the tabletop assembly from the frame and put two 1 1/2-inch screws through each of the blocks into the bottom of the tabletops. Predrill the screw holes with a countersink bit.

7. Attach the chain to the eyebolts by prying the edge of the eyebolt open just enough to slip one of the links of the chain through. Close again tightly.
8. Replace the tabletop assemblies over the ends of the tee fittings. For an even more secure table assembly, hold in place with a 1¹/₂-inch screw through the side of each of the blocks under the table.

Chair and sling

9. Next, dry-assemble the chair pieces. I suggest you break the assembly into three categories: the back, the bottom, and the sides. Start with the back pieces and assemble the unit on a flat level surface (FIG. 17-4). Assemble the bottom next (FIG. 17-5), and then the sides (FIG. 17-6).

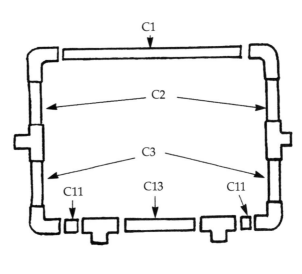

Fig. 17-4. Assemble the seat back with the pieces shown.

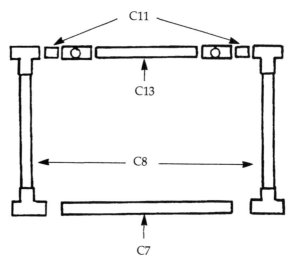

Fig. 17-5. Assemble the seat base with the pieces shown.

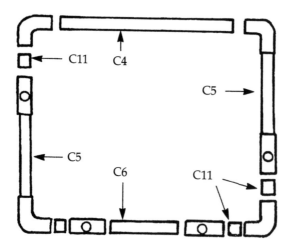

Fig. 17-6. Assemble the seat sides with the pieces shown, making two mirror-image sides.

10. Measure and cut the sling from the canvas. Hem the sides of the sling so the piece is 18 inches wide. Make 7-inch loops at each end, double-stitching the seam. The total length should be 43 inches from the end of each loop. From the excess, make 2 ties, 1×12 inches, to be sewn into the seam to secure canvas to the center pipe. See FIG. 17-7.

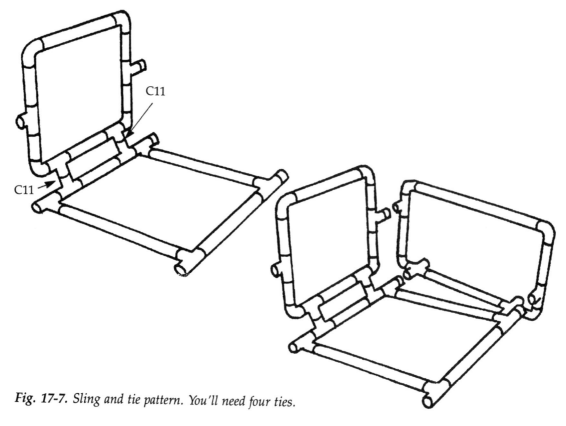

Fig. 17-7. Sling and tie pattern. You'll need four ties.

11. Put the back, bottom, and side assemblies together (FIG. 17-8), and attach the sling to the top and front center pieces as shown in FIG. 17-9.

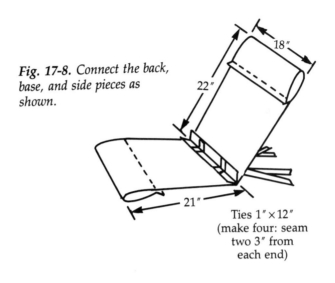

Fig. 17-8. *Connect the back, base, and side pieces as shown.*

18"

22"

21"

Ties 1" × 12"
(make four: seam
two 3" from
each end)

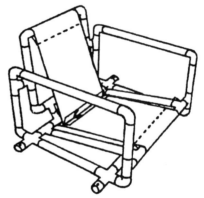

Fig. 17-9. *Don't forget to add the sling before the final assembly.*

12. Once you are certain the pieces all fit correctly and the unit sits flat, knock apart and then reassemble all but the top and front center pieces using cement.
13. Center and drill 3/8-inch holes in the chair's end caps. Insert the eyebolts with nuts and lock washers. Pry the ends of the eyebolts open and attach to the chain link from the frame. See FIG. 17-10. Reclose the eyebolts tightly.
14. Add a patio chair cushion, and swing to your heart's content.

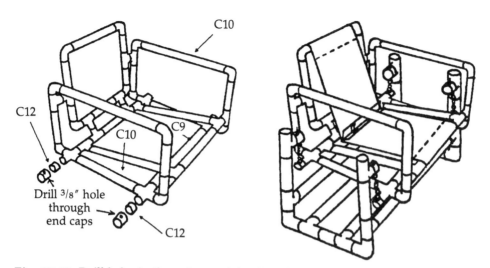

Fig. 17-10. Drill holes in the end caps of the chair frame (left) and attach to the base with chains (right).

18
Modular bookcase

Another shelving project suitable for any room in your home, this design can be used outdoors, too. With extra end caps, it can be separated into two shorter units to complement lawn chairs as side tables. Making the frame takes less than a hour.

Materials

- 1^1/$_2$-inch PVC pipe, 40 feet long (1^1/$_8$-inch fitting allowance), cut to size as follows:

  6 pieces 31 inches long (P1)
  4 pieces 12 inches long (P2)
  6 pieces 11 inches long (P3)
  4 pieces 10^1/$_2$ inches long (P4)
  12 pieces 8 inches long (P5)
  8 pieces 2^1/$_4$ inches long (P6)

- 1^1/$_2$-inch fittings:

  24 tees
  8 end caps

Hardware and miscellaneous

- 6 shelves, laminated white pine, 1×16×36 inches
- PVC cleaner
- Wood stain and sealer, or paint

Tools required

- Handsaw
- Square
- Saber saw
- Sandpaper
- Paintbrush

Instructions

Bookcase

1. Measure, cut, and label the straight pipe pieces as listed.
2. Dry-assemble the fittings and pipe pieces that form the bookcase frame as shown in FIG. 18-1.
3. Remove any marks from the pipe. I found this project did not require cement or fasteners. It is very sturdy regardless, and thus remains available for re-arranging.
4. The shelf corners will have to be notched to fit around the PVC frame. To mark the notches, lay each shelf on the floor and place a bookcase section over it. Trace around the fitting at each corner (FIG. 18-2).
5. Cut out the notches with a saber saw.
6. Sand and finish your shelves. Allow to dry thoroughly before inserting into the frame.

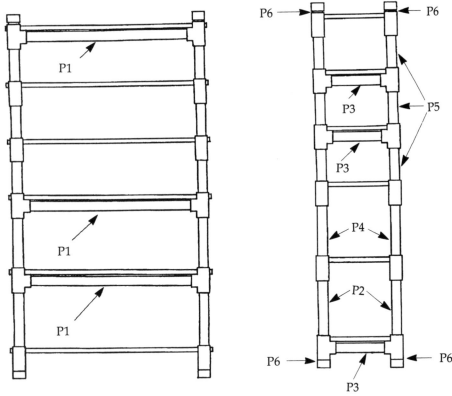

Fig. 18-1. Side (left) and front (right) views of the bookcase assembly. Note: P6 pieces are not shown in this illustration; insert them where indicated.

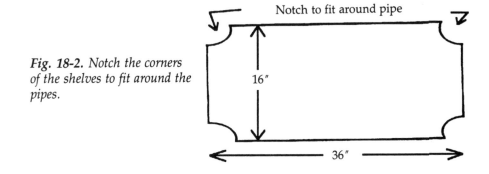

Fig. 18-2. Notch the corners of the shelves to fit around the pipes.

Notch to fit around pipe

16"

36"

7. While the shelves are drying, position your bookcase frame where you want it. After the shelves are in, this project is too heavy to move.
8. With eight additional end caps, you can create two shorter units.

19

Computer console

This project is one that will make your computer look right at home. It is designed to hold your computer and all of the necessary books and printers and other accessories that go with it. I painted this project black, but you can paint it the color of your choice.

Materials

- 1¹/₂-inch PVC pipe, 87 feet (1-inch fitting allowance), cut to size as follows:
  5 pieces 55¹/₂ inches long (P1)
  5 pieces 29 inches long (P2)
  3 pieces 37¹/₂ inches long (P3)
  1 piece 25¹/₂ inches long (P4)
  1 piece 24³/₄ inches long (P5)
  8 pieces 19 inches long (P6)
  8 pieces 20³/₄ inches long (P7)
  2 pieces 19 inches long (P8)
  4 pieces 6¹/₂ inches long (P9)
  25 pieces 2 inches long (P10)
  2 pieces 6¹/₂ inches long (P11)
  2 pieces 6¹/₄ inches long (P12)

- 1¹/₂-inch fittings:
  14 elbows, 90 degrees
  10 elbows, 45 degrees
  28 tees
  2 double tees

- ³/₄-inch red oak plywood, cut to size as follows:
  1 piece 28×32 inches
  1 piece 28×87¹/₂ inches

- ³/₄-inch red oak lumber, cut to size as follows:
  1 piece 10×43 inches, middle shelf
  1 piece 9×36 inches, left top shelf
  1 piece 9×37¹/₂ inches, middle top shelf
  1 piece 9×62¹/₂ inches, right top shelf
  2 pieces ³/₄×28 inches, trim
  1 piece ³/₄×32 inches, trim
  1 piece ³/₄×43³/₄ inches, trim
  1 piece ³/₄×32¹/₂ inches, trim
  1 piece ³/₄×60 inches, trim
  1 piece ³/₄×57³/₄ inches trim

Hardware and miscellaneous

- 30 drywall screws, 1¹/₄-inch
- 30 red oak wood plugs, ¹/₂-inch
- 4 pieces ¹/₄-inch plywood, 1×3 inches
- PVC cement
- Danish oil stain, walnut color
- PVC cleaner
- 1 quart undercoat paint

- 1 quart brown enamel
- 16 sheet-metal screws, 3/4-inch

Tools required

- Drill with 1/2-inch countersink bit
- Flap-wheel sander
- Table or radial arm saw
- Belt sander
- Screwdriver
- Handsaw
- Paintbrush

Instructions

This project is built in two units, the left side and the right side. It is then assembled with the center back connecting PVC pipe pieces, the desktop, and the shelving.

Frame

1. Measure, cut, and label the pipe pieces as listed.
2. Dry-assemble the left and right facing sides of each unit as shown in FIG. 19-1. Attach the center pipe P1 for the right side and P2 for the left side. Make certain the units are flat on the ground and do not wobble.
3. Knock apart and then reassemble each unit using PVC cement.
4. Attach both units at the two tee joints with one P10 piece. Do not cement the pipe yet.
5. Dry-assemble center connecting pipe and fittings as shown in FIG. 19-2. Attach the 45-degree elbows with pieces of P10 for the top and bottom, and P13 for the center shelf. Attach the PVC pipes marked P3, P4, and P5.
6. Once you are convinced the desk is assembled properly, knock apart and then reassemble the center pieces with PVC cement.
7. Remove all markings with PVC cleaner. If you wish to paint the desk, roughen the pipe and fittings with a flap-wheel sander. Apply the base or primer coat and allow to dry. Finish with the paint color of your choice.
8. Measure and cut all of the red oak plywood and lumber pieces to size. See FIG. 19-3.
9. Attach the 3/4-inch wood strips to the two 3/4-inch plywood pieces that will form the desktop. Glue the strips and hold in place with countersunk 1 1/4-inch screws. Glue and clamp the two desktop pieces together and hold in place with two strips of 1/4-inch plywood attached on the bottom and held in place with 3/4-inch wood screws. Allow to dry thoroughly.
10. Measure and cut the 3/4-inch red oak lumber to shape for the middle and top shelves.

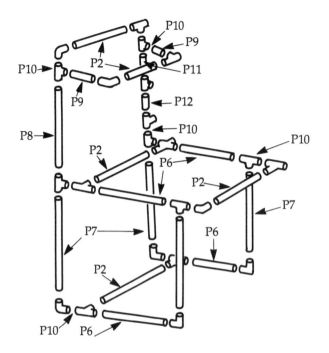

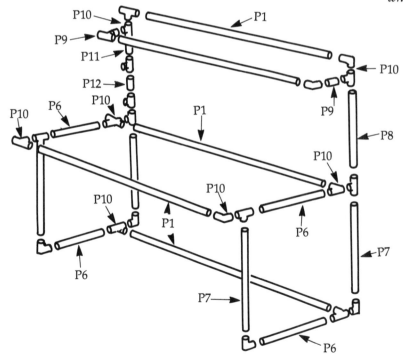

Fig. 19-1. *Assemble the left (top) and right (bottom) sides with the pieces shown. Note: P10 pieces are not shown in this illustration; insert them where indicated.*

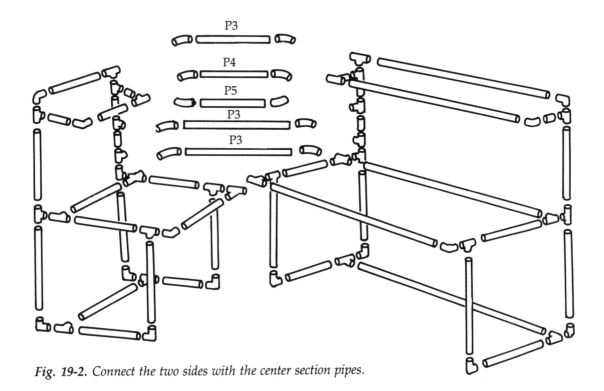

P3

P4

P5

P3

P3

Fig. 19-2. Connect the two sides with the center section pipes.

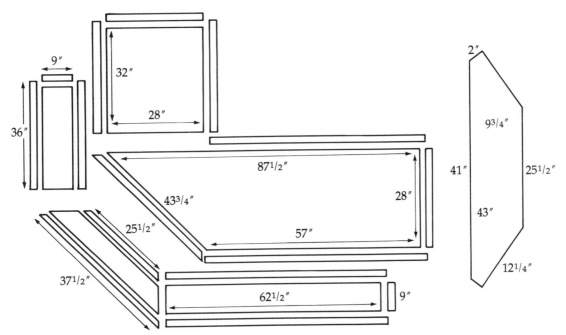

9″

32″

28″

36″

87¹/₂″

43³/₄″

28″

25¹/₂″

57″

37¹/₂″

62¹/₂″

9″

2″

9³/₄″

41″

25¹/₂″

43″

12¹/₄″

Fig. 19-3. Cut the plywood desktop and shelf pieces to the indicated sizes.

11. Lay the top shelving onto the top ledge of the desk. Attach the middle top board to the two end boards with two strips of $1/4$-inch plywood, glue, and $3/4$-inch wood screws.
12. Stain the desktop and the shelving with Danish oil in the color of your choice.

Chair

13. The instructions for the assembly of the chair are the same as the those presented in Project 12.

Making money building PVC furniture

Now that you have seen how simple and easy it is to make PVC pipe furniture, why not make some for somebody else and earn money in the process? Potential project ideas are unlimited. While I have shown you how to make 19 projects in this book, many more can be created and sold to individuals in your neighborhood or through retail stores, and even through the mail.

Some other project ideas include the following items that can be manufactured and sold as finished projects or in kit form:

- Doghouse frame
- Cat litter box cover frame
- Recycling center
- Bookcases
- Picture frames
- Pickup truck railings
- Headboards for beds
- Trivets
- Ladders
- Children's overhead bars
- Plant stands
- Tent frames
- Plant trellises
- TV stands
- Hammocks
- Sign holders
- Fence posts
- Mailboxes
- Bar stools
- Greenhouse frames
- Children's playhouse frames
- Storage shed frames
- Clothesline poles
- Birdhouses and feeders
- Gliders
- Food-serving carts
- Light fixtures

This list is actually small; let your own imagination roam and see how many different ideas you can come up with. PVC projects are simple to make and easily started in the basement or garage workshop with minimal investment in time or energy.

Starting your own business can be lots of fun, but also a big headache if you don't do it right. There is money to be made building PVC pipe projects, but you need to think about some basic things.

Sources of raw materials

Getting to know your local plumber is one way to start. Ask for leftover pipe from construction sites. Check with building contractors for the same reason. Offer to haul off the leftover pipe they usually toss out.

You'll probably find several sources of regular PVC pipe used for plumbing. Furniture-grade requires special fittings. Start by checking with your local plumbing wholesaler to learn what is available locally. Some other sources to check with include the following companies who can also lead you to other sources in their industry.

GENOVA PRODUCTS INC.
7034 E. Court St.
Davison, MI 48423-0309

LEISURE PRODUCTS
Box 3171
Apollo Beach, FL 33570

WENDELLYN INC.
15882 Manufacture Ln.
Huntington Beach, CA 62649

U.S. PLASTICS CORP.
1390 Neubrecht Rd.
Lima, OH 45801

For plans and patterns for other PVC designs, you can write to Baldwin Publishing Inc., Eureka, MO 63025. The catalog is $3.00.

For cushions and other attachments to furniture, you can start out by making your own. Hiring high-school students who have taken sewing lessons in home-economics classes is one way to start. Pay them by the piece however, not by the hour. Check with the local home centers that sell replacement lawn furniture cushions. Find out where they buy their products; what are their sources of supply? Check with wholesalers in your area that supply upholstery material to furniture rebuilders. Other potential sources include:

HOOVER INDUSTRIES
7260 N.W. 68th St.
Miami, FL 33152

INTERNATIONAL CUSHION CO.
1110 N.E. 8th Ave.
Ft. Lauderdale, FL 33304

Marketing, advertising and promotion

The most important thing you have to do in starting any new business is defining your market. Put simply, who would want to buy your product? Where are they located? The next step is to decide the best way to communicate the availability of your product to these potential buyers.

Advertising can be expensive. Small businesses have to learn to be innovative and creative in order to get recognition for their products. For a surprisingly simple way to get free advertising, read on.

Your local newspaper is always interested in an enterprising story. Create a news release that sounds important, one that tells all about your new company and how important your new products are. Don't make it sales- or promotion-oriented, just tell the facts in an interesting and informative way. Treat it as though you are writing a feature story. Send copies to your local newspapers—dailies, weeklies, and the special free publications such as the classified shoppers. Send copies to all of the TV stations and radio stations in your area. Find out who the key editor is and address it to him or her personally. Include a high-quality photograph of some of your products to illustrate how good they look.

This story might be picked up and run as a news feature, or the TV or radio stations might send a reporter to talk to you. Pick a time when there is a lull in national or local news. Don't send out your news release right after a flood, the death of an important figure, or an international incident. Timing is all-important in getting your message read and used. This free advertising could open some very important doors for you and make you a lot of money.

Creating a good story about your product is important. Many people miss the boat because they don't do their homework and plan an effective campaign. What are the features, functions, and benefits of your product? Why should people spend money on your product? What is in it for them? You must have a good story about why your product is so fantastic?

Promotions and crazy gimmicks help attract a crowd. Get permission from a local home center to stage a promotion in its parking lot over a weekend. After all, it will help the store sell products, too.

Word of mouth is perhaps the best and cheapest of all advertising. Pick a project that is really needed and fill that need, and you will go to the bank with the results.

I'm sure if you think it through, you too, can come up with lots of ways to promote and advertise your new product and make lots of money.

Selling and distributing your products

Here are but a few of the many ways that you can sell and distribute your products and make money:

- Selling your products can be as simple as staging a garage sale or buying space at a flea market. I know lots of people who regularly pick up thousands of dollars every year selling this way on a part-time basis. They keep their regular jobs and make extra money on weekends. Make up brochures about your products and hand them out. People who didn't buy this week might come back next week.
- Sell your products wholesale to retailers. Just look in the yellow pages of the phone book for the furniture dealers, home centers, and swimming pool suppliers in your area. They are all candidates for your products.
- Consigning your products through retailers is another way to make money, and is also a good way to start with retailers. Once they see how well the product sells, they are apt to come back to you for a large wholesale order.
- Go talk to developers of condos and apartment complexes in your area to develop a list of the people renting or buying from them who might be customers for your products.
- Mail-order is another way of selling your product. It involves some risk, but if you tap into the right market, it could prove to be enormously profitable. Many books are available that can teach you about direct-mail marketing.

- Swimming pool owners are prime candidates for PVC furniture. It looks great at poolside, it's easy to maintain, and it's almost indestructible.
- Volunteer your products for window dressings at department stores. Make certain you get credit so people will know about you.

Business basics and record keeping

The first lesson in any business is to grow slowly. You can start working out of your home and gradually expand to larger facilities once you have the sales volume to justify the move. Think small and keep your overhead low. Learn to grow by the bootstrap method. Don't buy anything until you absolutely need it. Never spend money on anything that will not directly make money for you.

Don't borrow money unless you know the loan is going into something with an immediate payback. Repay the loan as soon as possible. Don't buy equipment, trucks, copying machines or anything that you can obtain by using someone else's service. Spending five cents for a copy when you need it beats having to pay off a $5,000 loan for a copying machine.

In general, be very careful about how you spend your money. If you do have to buy anything, such as a computer for keeping records, lease it, don't buy it. Always protect your cash reserves and make your money work for you.

Keep accurate records of all transactions. Keep them separate from your personal bills and receipts. Do not mix your business with your personal transactions.

Check with a lawyer for the pros and cons of incorporating your business in your state. Incorporating can protect you from such things as business bankruptcy, tax avoidance, business liabilities, etc. Drawbacks to incorporating include strict state laws governing business, requirements for elaborate bookkeeping procedures, reports to state and local governments, and, in some states, higher taxes.

Find a competent CPA or bookkeeper who specializes in working with small businesses. Go to your local bookstore and buy some books about starting your own business and read them thoroughly.

Develop a trade name for your company, a "doing-business-as" name that identifies your company and what it does or is. Your trade name is the basic identity that all of your customers will relate to. Adopting a trade name will also make it easier for you to keep your personal and business transactions separate.

Be careful about mixing business and pleasure. Be very careful about involving your spouse or children in the company with you. Few families can do so successfully, and it could mean the end of your marriage if things do not work out. If you plan to work out of your home, check out the local ordinances.

Get to know your banker. Get him or her involved with you right up front. Keep a second bank in mind when you do so. I suggest you find the smallest bank in your area so that you can get to know the key people immediately. Establish a line of credit by borrowing money when you don't need it and then paying it back before the due date. Continue to take out loans, increasing the amount you borrow each time, until you have a reliable line of credit for when you really do need it.

Find good sources of supply and maintain good relations with your suppliers and creditors. Pay everybody on time, and don't ignore problems when they occur, since they usually do not go away and only compound in time.

Go see the Small Business Administration. The SBA offers free seminars, books, brochures, and counseling that can help. It also can help with financing in some cases.

Remember that it takes money to make money. If you don't have at least some capital, you're not going to get very far. Also remember that nothing is going to happen until you sell something. You might have the greatest ideas in the world, but they are worthless until someone else buys them.

Manufacturing and pricing

You can make most PVC projects with ordinary hand tools. As your business starts to grow, you most certainly will want to add power tools to increase the output.

One tool that you can make is a cut-off tool for cutting straight pipe to length. An ordinary hand-held circular saw can be used for this purpose if you are creative. A radial arm saw is also a tool that will come in handy.

A large, wide, flat work area is also needed. You can make this by mounting a piece of 4-×-8 plywood, 3/4 inch thick, on saw horses or on a 2-×-4 frame.

If your project requires a lot of drilling, an investment in a stationary drill press will also be necessary. A bench-top model should be more than adequate.

Pricing your product is going to be a bit tricky. You have to decide what you want for your time and labor, your overhead, and your out-of-pocket raw material costs. Factoring in what the market will bear will help you decide what kind of profit you want to make.

A rule of thumb is to make at least twice what your known direct costs were. If you are adding a lot of value to your pieces, through decorative painting, or are creating a unique project, of course, the pricing can be what the market will bear. If you choose to go with volume, the pricing can be lower.

Opportunity exits in every situation in life. Even when situations and things really seem in the pits, you can find a way out and a way to prosper. You are the sum total of your very own thoughts and experiences. You have choices in life: making the right choices is up to you. Making PVC projects is one way for a small business to grow into a large one. It depends, by and large, on your own initiative, creativity, and hard work to succeed. In purchasing this book you have taken the very first step.

Index

One Final Note

I hope that you enjoyed building these projects as well as the other projects from my syndicated newspaper columns and PBS programs. If you need full size patterns, or if you would like to see some of the other projects we make, send $3.00 for our catalog. If you have any questions about this book, or if you need help, write to my attention, and we will get back to you as soon as possible. Our address is:

The Weekend Workshop
P.O. Box 40
Eureka, Missouri 63025

And remember, you really can make it!